Encyclopedia of Character

Steins

by Dr. Eugene Manusov

Library of Congress
Catalog Number 75 21330

ISBN: 0-87069-122-8

Published by
Wallace-Homestead Book Co.
Box BI
Des Moines, Iowa 50304

Printed in U.S.A.

CONTENTS

BIOGRAPHY

Born—Los Angeles, CA
Graduate University of Southern California, School of
    Dentistry.
Fellow of American Academy of General Dentistry.
Officer in USAF—Stationed in Japan for two years.
Past-President—"Erste Gruppe" So. Calif. component of
    Stein Collections Int'l.
Past-Chief-of-Staff, Santa Monica Hospital Dental Clinic.
Board of Directors of the Western Dental Society and
    Academy of General Dentistry.
HOBBIES—Stein-collecting, Photography, Traveling,
            Antiquing.

Have been collecting steins for over EIGHT years—Favorites
of course are Character Steins.

FOREWORD

Think, for a moment, of a cool, frothy stein of beer on a warm summer evening. Think of the *Gemutlichkeit* of sharing happy moments with friends and family. Somehow these thoughts seem to come to mind when I gaze at the Character Steins sitting on my shelves. I look at a tipsy monkey with his forlorn face, eyes peering with a glazed look, and I'm carried back in time to a more relaxed world. Or was it? I look at a skull with an inscription on the lid to a student long gone. Was school easier in those days? Maybe! All steins are like seashells, they seem to tell tales of years gone by. Hold your ear to an open stein. Can you hear a little singing in the *Hofbrauhaus?* I can. To me, though, there is a little something extra in a Character Stein. Sure, I love the beauty of a Schlitt Mettlach and an etched glass drinking vessel is a sight to behold. But a Character — ah, it's beauty and fun rolled into one little package.

I started this project a couple of years ago, thinking I could whip it out in no time at all. What fools we are at times! As the pictures poured in from throughout the country, I came to realize that there was no end to the ingenuity of the artisans of old. Every picture would send a ripple of excitement down my spine as I saw something new. I hope this book affects you similarly. Unfortunately, I had to stop somewhere. I am sure there are many, many more steins lurking in attics, sitting on mantles, hidden in closets, waiting to rattle my chromosomes when I see them. But alas, the time has come. Hopefully this little book will lead to others -- then we can show you more.

So what is a Character Stein? Many definitions have been given, but to me it is a stein having a shape other than cylindrical and representing an object, figure or caricature. The body and lid together make up the shape. It is capable of representing something to the observer without having to resort to relief, print under glaze, etched or painted decorations. We have not included, except for a few, steins that have lids in the shape of turret, tower, sport, or object. The steins with figural or character lids are intriguing, but would require an entire book in themselves.

I have tried to eliminate relatively new steins from this edition. However, I am aware that some are present. In recent years most German manufacturers have discontinued production of Character Steins due to their high cost, so the new steins of today may become collectible rapidly.

As you read through this book the descriptions may be redundant. For this I apologize. I have attempted to keep my verbiage to a minimum. Many details are obvious in the photos. This is primarily an illustrated encyclopedia, and I hope that is what my readers want. The next best thing to having and feeling the stein is seeing it, and that is what this book is all about. Having had the opportunity to examine many of the steins in this book, I have seen a great variety in coloring and details from stein to stein. In the 'old days' these steins were handcrafted, and therefore variances were the rule. If your stein does not match the illustration, don't get excited; I understand. That's what stein collecting is all about.

The same variations have been noted in the markings on the steins. Very often we have noted similar steins with different marks, both in the manufacturer and the various numbers on the bases. This we understand also. In my descriptions I refer to NO MARKS on many steins. That signifies no manufacturer's marks. Where the manufacturer is known, it is keyed to the section on marks and manufacturers.

The most fun of this book for me was the translation from Old German to modern day meaning. Many inscriptions were relating to a day long since past, time that not many of us have seen (although in my stein-listening I have heard). Many of the verses have been shortened due to space requirements on the steins. Many verses refer to folklore of years gone by. Many verses lose something in the translation. Thanks to the knowledge and fluency of Lotti Lopez and Don and Evelyn Sherman, some of the double (and triple) meanings have been unraveled. If our translations, descriptions, and interpretations raise a few eyebrows, I am glad. I hope this book will be as exciting to you, the reader, as it was to me.

I have not gone into great details concerning the backgrounds on many of these steins. They have been explored by many other fine writers. Those of you who are members of Stein Collectors International have read many articles on Character Steins in *Prosit.* Roland Henschen's "Steinmaker" articles in the *Tri-State Trader* are numerous. No one can write better than Terry Hill and his excellent articles. Jack Lowenstein, Dr. Joe Hersh, and others have published many extensive articles on the same subject. I hope we have added a little to what they have done in the past.

So, my friends, lift your steins on high -- gaze into the Happy Radish's smiling face. Certainly your drink will taste a wee bit better when he whispers something in your ear. Drink up and turn the page . . .

PROSIT!

Rubaiyat of Omar Khayyam; illustrated by Edmund J. Sullivan

ACKNOWLEDGMENTS

The photographs and descriptions in this book would never have been possible without the efforts of stein buffs the country over. The man who rates number one, and certainly should be co-author with me, is my dear buddy, Mike Wald. Without his cooperation in getting pictures and descriptions of the many fine collections in the East, this book would never have been written. He was most instrumental in getting permission to visit and photograph the collection that made a good book into, hopefully, a great book. That, of course, is the collection of the "Dean" himself, Bill Schwartz.

My gratitude to "Mr. Munich Child," Jack Lowenstein; to *Prosit* Editor, Jack Heimann, for allowing everyone who sent me photos to know that they were in safe hands (and for getting me his pictures just in time); to the "Seguin Cowboy," Fredlein Schroeder; and to the other Texan, Jim Hansen. My thanks are out to Roland Henschen for his fine chapter on the manufacture of Character Steins and his immeasurable help with the manufacturers and marks. If they are not right, blame Roland. Also a big *danke* to Norm Medow, Dick Ehlert, Jim Talley, Leonard Schenk, and Joe Hersh. The authenticity of the military attire is attributed to Eric Johansson, Editor of *Kaiserzeit.*

I have a special thank you for my fellow "Erste Gruppians" in California. Starting with Lotti and Victor Lopez and Terry Hill, the thanks are extended to our own "Bill Schwartz" -- Joe Durban and his *Frau,* Mary; our northern "Mr. Character Stein," Harry Carskadon; Frank Love; Bob and Ruthe White; Mario Pancino; Jon Rosenbaum; Mel Preszler; Al Edmonds; Don and Evelyn Sherman; and all the others who wish to remain anonymous.

Of course last, but certainly not least, my dear harem of Pat, Vicki, and Valerie, who spent many unnecessary Sundays at home while I cursed at the typewriter. I love you all.

Rubaiyat of Omar Khayyam; illustrated by Edmund J. Sullivan

WHY A CHARACTER STEIN?

by Jack G. Lowenstein

Man's earliest artistic instinct was somehow to copy and thus preserve what he saw in nature. Cave drawings depicting primitive attempts of this type of imagery have been uncovered all over the world. Little wonder then that the ancient clay worker also turned to nature for his models: the world around him — often difficult to comprehend — was reproduced in simple, understandable, and permanent forms, the clay worker's imagination limited only by the pliability of the clay in his hands. Countless examples of early pottery in the crude form of animals and humans attest to this beginning of the potter's art.

It wasn't long before our ancient clay worker tired of modeling little figurines and instead turned to making useful objects. Pots, dishes, bowls and other assorted utilitarian items replaced such natural objects as coconut shells, palm fronds, sea shells, and hollowed-out wood. But he never forgot his first love, and soon he found ways of combining his artistic copying with his more mundane work. The result, of course, was a utilitarian receptacle in the shape of an animal. Figural or character vessels had been invented!

As pottery and ceramics advanced and developed into full-blown forms of art, the concept of figurals also was perfected. Chinese porcelain figural vessels were produced as early as 200 B.C., Greek figural items as early as 1200 B.C., and Minoan items as early as 2000 B.C. In Europe, where the discovery of stoneware in the 13th century heralded a new era, figural vessels were known almost from the very beginning. As soon as the people of the Middle Ages found that the new stoneware items were able to hold liquids better than anything that came before (except expensive glass and metal), they began to artistically decorate the marvelous new mugs and tankards — and once again the figural model was re-born. The *Bartmann Krüge* ("Bellarmine jugs") of the early 16th century, the *Eulenkrüge* ("owl jugs") of the

mid-16th century, and the Medici "porcelain" figural ewers of the late 15th and early 16th centuries are probably the earliest examples of what might be classified as "character steins"; the famous Brixener *Eullenpokal* ("owl tankard") of about 1540 may, however, be the first true Character Stein (as proposed by Roland Henschen), since its purpose as a drinking vessel — rather than storage vessel — appears clear.

But the Character Stein didn't really come into its own until the 1850s, when a more relaxed way of living, combined with a German artists' renaissance and an emphasis on beautiful, unique, and sometimes personalized beer-drinking vessels, gave impetus to the design, manufacture, and widespread use of these ingenious steins.

Figural steins were shaped like animal or human heads, figurines, or other "characters". Whimsy naturally played a large part, and allegorical figures, animals with pseudo-human features, and popular or humorous figures were (and still are) great favorites. This book is a tribute to the vast imagination of the Character Stein designer, to the spectrum of characters turned into useful drinking vessels, and to the great humor and satire expressed in these clever figurals.

Let's discuss some of the better known "characters". The beer-drinking and beer-loving Germans even personified the condition of inebriation: To be drunk was to have a *Kater* ("tomcat"), and a hangover is known by the same name. Similarly, to have a monkey ("Affe") on one's back was to be a drunk. Spring beer is known as *Bock* ("ram" or "goat") *Bier;* to have good luck is to have *Schwein* ("pig"); as in the United States, to be clever is to be a "fox"; of course a night person is an "owl"; also a scholar might be termed an "owl". Thus the tomcat, the monkey, the goat, the pig, the fox, and the owl were early Character Stein favorites. They were given human features, clothes to wear, and pipes to smoke.

5

The owner of such a stein said, in effect, "Look here — I like my beer and I'm proud of it!"

Big, white radishes are the favorite beer snack in the Bavarian mountains. Thus the happy and the sad radish Character Steins were naturals. One radish was happy because he made the legendary Bavarian beer even more enjoyable, while the other one was sad because he foresaw his own early demise.

Hunting is a popular European sport. The Germans took hunting very seriously because game was so plentiful within their borders. And, after the hunt, what more pleasant pastime than to sit in the warm hunting lodge and swap some tall tales over a foaming stein or two? (Countless German paintings of the 19th century depict just such scenes.) It is quite obvious that the true *Kenner* ("connoisseur") would want to show off his hobby (hunting, not drinking). The result was Character Steins in the shape of stags, bears, boars, foxes, rabbits, and other assorted denizens of the forest. To minimize the idea that these animals were the "victims" of the sport, they were instead often depicted as the hunters themselves — they were given human features, "wore" hunting clothes, and carried guns. After all, what could be a slyer dig than a stein in the shape of a rabbit, walking on his hind legs, dressed as a hunter with gun over shoulder, and carrying a game sack out of which peeked a small human being?

The mere thought of drinking out of a skull has intrigued man for centuries. Monks were often accused of this grisly custom in the Middle Ages by the ignorant and the malicious. Little wonder, then, that a skull Character Stein should appear! Being made of stoneware or pottery, instead of bone, it legitimatized the hidden, morbid desires. Indeed, it made fun of them. Thus we find skull steins of all types: osteologically correct skulls; skulls resting on books (variously inscribed seriously or humorously -- *Gaudeamus Igitur* ("So let us be joyful") seems to be a favorite); skulls with ravens on top; skulls with an ancient candle on top of the cranium; even skulls which, when turned around, revealed a grinning devil. Once the initial revulsion was overcome, the imagination of the stein designer seemed to have no limits.

The devil himself was a fascinating model for the Character Stein maker; *zum Teufel* is a favorite German expletive (not always deleted), and someone who drank too much was — according to some — surely on his way to the netherworld and its fiery, horned, and tailed master. Hence what better figural out of which to drink one's beer? Like the skull, the devil steins come in many configurations, from stern, threatening, and frightening to scowling, enticing, and downright lovable.

But there are probably no better-known Character Steins than the Munich Child steins! The *Münchner*

Kindl, as it is known in its home town of Munich, is the beloved symbol of that fair city and Bavaria. Created as the coat-of-arms or archival seal of Munich in 1239, it has evolved from a hooded monk standing in front of Munich's gate to a charming child (almost always depicted as female), still dressed in hood and cape but now holding a foaming stein of beer and a bunch of radishes instead of the Book of Law. A most impressive history of the metamorphosis of the Munich Child was written by Ernst von Destouches in 1905. The change from monk to child was slow and almost imperceptible; by 1865 the official seal of Munich was represented by a youngish figure with definite religious overtones (red halo, right hand extended in blessing). Yet the new post-war seal has returned to the monk figure, stylized but recognizable.

It was up to the artists, the painters, the sculptors, the printers to transform the seal-figure into the beer drinker's Munich child. In the second half of the 19th century the fun-figure emerged — always holding that stein — and at once it became the "official" symbol of all *Münchner* ("citizens of Munich"). The Child found its way to posters, to paintings, to newspaper mastheads, to calendars, to all types of decorative articles, and, naturally, to beer steins. Literally thousands of different Munich Child representations were immortalized on PUG; painted, relief, and etched stoneware; porcelain; glass; and pewter steins! Little wonder then that Munich Child character steins were not far behind. The figure is easy to model and artistic possibilities are limitless. Famous stoneware and porcelain workers, such as Martin Pauson, Josef Reinemann, and Josef M. Mayer (all of Munich), turned out wondrous arrays of Munich Child Character Steins. Some were made of stoneware, others of porcelain (sometimes with lovely, almost life-like bisque faces), and still others of pewter. Almost every stein manufacturer (with the notable absence of Villeroy & Boch) tried his hand at a Munich Child character or two, all with unique features of style, from the 1870s to the present, which accounts for the large number of these characters still being found. From the cherubic to the irreverent, from the ultimate in refinement to the common and crude, the Munich Child Character Stein is instantly recognized by every serious collector by its hood, its robe with cross-shaped belt, the radishes, and the ever-present foaming stein.

Character Steins portraying nuns and monks are a cross between sly mockery and good-natured humor. No harm was ever intended by these little figurals. Besides, how could anyone ever take a beer drinker seriously?

Even famous people were immortalized on Character Steins: President Otto von Bismarck; Field Marshall Paul von Hindenburg; both Kaisers Wilhelm (I and II); Count Ferdinand von Zeppelin; Uncle Sam; the Wright brothers. They all found their way into this form of sculpture. Here no mockery was intended. The owner of a Character Stein depicting a real person was showing his respect, his true liking for the person, whether past or present. (Frank Love has done extensive research on the subject "Steins as Portraits" and perhaps he will soon publish a definitive work on this interesting side-light.)

The jump from representing real people to imaginary ones was easy, and therefore you will see in this book a large number of "people" figurals. Men and women from all stages of life, from all professions, from mythology and from folk-tales, or just from the imagination of the stein manufacturer, can be found in the form of steins. Here we see finely detailed sculptures or crude imagery. Whether the Character Stein represents the ever-maligned mother-in-law or the sexy barmaid, the chivalrous gentleman or the rascally imbiber, a servant girl or a mountaineer, an Indian or the Heidelberg dueling student, the humor, the cleverness, and the fancy are always apparent to the viewer. Often a line or two of text on the stein relates the figure to some aspect of life, mostly beer drinking. (The German texts are often arduous and tortured to form a rhyme or to fit the space. Therefore they are sometimes difficult to translate or even to understand. The combination of poetic license and local dialects can easily defeat the translator. If nothing else, the literal translation often completely misses the point of humor and hence becomes senseless.)

The variety of Character Steins certainly seems endless. It is just about impossible to verbally catalogue every item -- a "trip" through this book is necessary to convince oneself of the magnitude of Character Stein types.

Only one final Character Stein deserves detailed comments: *der Nürnberger Trichter* ("the Nuremberg Funnel"). Although Nuremberg is represented in the world of steins by its famous tower and by the Goose Man, it is the Funnel which is the enigma. The tower, of course, is the *Spittlertortum* ("Spittler Gate Tower"), one of the six towers surrounding Nuremberg, and the Goose Man is a figure from one of that city's famous fountains. But the Funnel — just what does it mean? What does it represent? Several variations of the funnel stein are known. One is in the form of the funnel itself (with jester handle), another features the funnel as a man's hat, while a third shows the funnel as being used (again, by a jester) to pour something into a fool's head. Our guess is that the funnel is used to funnel knowledge! The clue lies in a

Rubaiyat of Omar Khayyam; **illustrated by Edmund J. Sullivan**

postcard (discovered by Frank Love) which shows the funnel being utilized to infuse a potion into a young man, while the text states: "Der Nürnberger Trichter — Sicher and schnell — Macht er die Köpfe hell!" The translation is: "The Nuremberg funnel: Surely and quickly -- it makes heads bright!" This ties in with the figure of the jester (the court fool) and the dumb expression on the figure being "infiltrated". There may well be other theories, but for the time being this one appears to be the most reasonable.

Much could still be said about the variety of thumb-lifts and lithophanes found on and in Character Steins. The thumb-lifts, cast in pewter, often match the motif of the stein (such as the use of the twin towers of Munich's Cathedral of Our Lady on Munich Child steins, or the above-mentioned Goose Man on Nuremberg Tower steins), or else are one of a myriad of decorative designs. Lithophanes, those translucent pictoral bases in steins which become visible when the empty stein is held against the light, usually mirror some aspect of the stein itself or the location where the stein was made or sold. Thus, military figurals will feature a lithophane depicting a soldier, an officer, or another military personality. Munich Child steins most often have lithophanes showing the famous Bavaria statue on the Theresien Meadow in Munich. Nuremberg steins show the Nuremberg castle or one of the well-known, ornate Nuremberg fountains. Heidelberg steins will usually have a lithophane of the Heidelberg castle, high above the Rhine. On the other hand, many of the lithophanes in character steins are of the "general" variety: a girl reading a letter from a boy friend; a group of men playing cards; a family scene in front of a fireplace; a shepherd and shepherdess exchanging a kiss; and other similarly bucolic scenes. (Interestingly, beer steins were always considered "family-type" items -- hence risque or indecent lithophanes are exceedingly rare! Even the socially acceptable artistic female nude is only very rarely encountered. Hence we might say that beer steins, especially Character Steins, could be rated "PG").

Since one comes across the same lithophane views again and again, often in rather dissimilar steins by different manufacturers, one might assume that lithophanes were manufactured centrally and then purchased by stein manufacturers to be "inserted" into porcelain steins. Alternately, perhaps the lithophane molds were sold to the stein makers, to be used as the matrix from which to form the final translucent base panel. This common thread seems to run through all lithophaned porcelain steins, whether from the factory of Josef Mayer or the mysterious factory using the " # " and "Musterschutz" designations.

Character steins came into being and are collectible even today because they are artistic, they depict the humorous side of life, sometimes they have a tale to tell, they express a whimsy, a fantasy — yes, a *Gemutlichkeit* which we find enjoyable and which we attempt to duplicate vicariously by collecting them. In addition, they make great conversation pieces when stacked on a shelf, they spur research into an almost forgotten past, they fulfill our urge to collect, and last, but not least, they make beer taste better and even more fun to drink.

Rubaiyat of Omar Khayyam; illustrated by Edmund J. Sullivan

MANUFACTURING OF CHARACTER STEINS

by Roland A. Henschen

In this chapter we are mainly discussing production in a period dating back from World War II, and, more specifically, from around 1850 to 1930, with the bulk of the better characters made before World War I. I must, to accomplish my goal in the space permitted, speak with many generalities. I will ask that the reader appreciate the fact that while much is written of the production of porcelain and stoneware, little has been published applying this production to beer steins in general, and less to Character Steins in particular. To do a complete and thorough job would require many volumes, because we would have to take into consideration all the various techniques and variations used and developed by each of the many makers of Character Steins, not to mention the various influences of the prevailing art styles, along with the techniques and aesthetic demands of the time period involved. Nor will we attempt to discuss the various historical developments and influences leading up to this time period.

While Character Steins have been made of almost every material, the majority of the ones available for collection seem to be of three types: (1) porcelain; (2) *Feinsteinzeug,* ("fine stoneware"); and (3) one that greatly resembles bone china, being thinner and lighter than porcelain and more vulnerable to damage or breakage.

The Character Stein, as any other stein, has its beginnings with a designer or modeler and is formed or modeled on the work table from drawings and sketches made by the designer. These may be original ideas, characters from real life, historical characters, drawn from art works, and variations of another artist's works. Many characters are related to German drinking life. Simple forms are often completed quite quickly, while I also know of one stein (not a character) which required fifteen months for the modeler to complete. From this model a mold of plaster is made. On Character Stein molds it was often necessary to omit outstanding features which protruded greatly from the stein: these had to be applied by hand later. In some ways it is a shame that the days of this one-man or family pottery -- where the craftsman did all of the jobs -- gave way to industrialization before most of the Character Steins were made. If it had not, however, we would not have so many Character Steins to collect and appreciate. We may also take comfort in knowing that many characters were produced in shops of less than ten workers, where the master could carefully check the quality.

The next step in production is naturally the clay. In earlier times potters attempted to find a single clay that was suitable for use without mixing. This one clay from an open pit mine would be delivered directly to the pottery where it would be worked into a workable consistency, in older times by hand, today by machine. If water was added to help purify the clay, then the clay had to be thoroughly kneaded and squeezed to remove water and air. In porcelain, other materials were added so that a typical porcelain body composition might be: clay, 54%; flint, 25%; feldspar, 20%; whiting, 1%.

After the clay was properly prepared, it had to be pressed into the mold. While a few of the Character Steins may have been thrown on the wheel, it is a pretty safe bet that most were formed by casting in a mold. Most of these were three-piece molds, although there were a few four-piece molds. The two-piece mold was eliminated because the high relief of Character Steins made it unsuitable for use. At one time the pressing of the clay in the mold was done entirely by hand on a wheel, but over the years machinery took over this job.

If the mold was an extremely complicated one, another method was used to cast. In this method clay was mixed with water until it was able to be poured. The plaster mold was then filled with this mixture, called "slip". As the water was absorbed by the mold's porous wall, a clay crust was formed against the walls of the mold. When this crust was of the desired thickness, the center was poured off. The mold was removed, leaving the raw Character Stein body.

Because some of the steins had outstanding features, such as nose, ears, trunks, etc., protruding from the body, it is likely, in many cases, that these features were not made as part of the mold, but were added by hand after the original forming in the mold, much as the handle of the stein was applied separately. So skillfully could this application be accomplished, that it was as impossible in many steins to see this joining as it was to see the mold seams.

It is also easy to see that often much handwork was done after the mold was removed, to make the special features (hands, eyebrows, beards, etc.) as prominent, clear, and definite as they are. This is especially noticeable when compared with lower quality steins of yesterday and today.

Many questions have been asked about the firing. Some claim the steins were produced in a single firing, but this was not the German way. Most factories bisque-fired first; next they decorated; then they applied the glaze; and finally fired the piece. It was not uncommon to see a large jug-shaped, wood-fired furnace, in which the steins were bisqued in the upper chamber and final fired in the lower.

Most of the old Character Steins produced up to the 1930s were fired by one of the following methods: (1) by wood only; (2) by coal only, and (3) by a combination of wood and a pressed coal briquet (not coke).

Contrary to present day claims, I believe a person well acquainted with firing can determine the difference between a piece fired by the above mentioned materials and one fired by the present-day gas, oil, and electricy.

Ceramic lids were made in the same general way, to be attached in a number of ways to the body by a pewter hinge.

If the stein was to be completed with one firing and the decoration was to be all underglaze (underglaze decoration seemed to be the most popular in Character Steins), then all of the paint had to be applied before firing. The delicate condition of the clay coming directly to the decorator from the mold called for much skill and a delicate touch. Most German decorators demanded at least a period of air drying, although they preferred a bisque firing. After the bisque decorating was applied, a proper glaze was applied and the stein was high-temperature fired to vitrify. Since not all colors could stand the high fire necessary for vitrification, and since it was often desired to add other colors, it was then necessary to repeat the process; that is, to add the new colors and fire at a lower temperature. Sometimes on a better Character Stein, this might be repeated three or four times with a lower temperature each time.

The glaze may have been applied to the Character Stein by dipping or by brush. In the case of salt-glazed steins, salt was introduced in the furnace. Equal results were obtained by either method, but Character Stein makers seemed to prefer the dipping as being faster. We sometimes find the glaze was even sprayed on.

A complete explanation cannot be accomplished in so brief a chapter, but I sincerely hope that this will serve to help the reader to obtain some insight into the complexities of Character Stein production.

MARKS AND MANUFACTURERS

(1a) **PORZELLANMANUFAKTUR PLAUE**
The HASH or TIC-TAC-TOE mark is one of several used by this company from Thuringia (1817-present). This firm is believed to be the only one still manufacturing lithophanes. Located in East Germany (DDR).

(1b) SCHIERHOLZ & SOEHNE of Plaue.

(2) **E. BOHNE SOEHNE**
Rudolstadt, Thuringa (1854-after 1900).

(a)　　　(b)　　　(c)

(3) **D.R.G.M. (DEUTCHES REICHS-GEBRAUCHMUSTER)**
Means design is registered or patented. Pre-1918.

(4) **MERKELBACH & WICK**
Now known as WICK-WERKE of Höhr-Grenzhausen.

(4a) 1872-1921

Wick-Werke Wick-Werke W

(4b) 1921-1937　　(4c) 1937-1960　　(4d) Since 1960　　(4e)

11

(5)   REINHOLD-MERKELBACH of Höhr-Grenzhausen

(5a)   1870-1933   (5b)   1912-1925

(5c)   1925-1945

(5d)   1945-1964

(5e)   1964-1968

(5f)   Since 1968

(6)   ECKHARDT & ENGLER KG
       From Höhr-Grenzhausen. Founded in 1898. The firm went out of production in 1972.
       The KG refers to Kommandit Gesenschaft (limited partnership).

(6a)   (6b)

(7)   ALBERT JACOB THEWALT of Höhr-Grenzhausen

(7a)   1893-1896   (7b)   1897-1920   (7c)   1920-1930   (7d)   Since 1930

(8)   SIMON PETER GERZ
       Of Sessenbach and Höhr-Grenzhausen. Founded 1862.

(9)   MARZI & REMI
      From Höhr-Grenzhausen. Founded 1879.

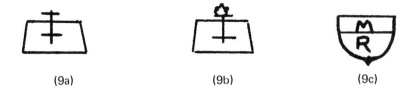

            (9a)   (9b)   (9c)

(10) MUSTERSCHUTZ
      Means Registered design; Trademark; Patent; Copyright and Model protection.

                                                    „musterschutz"

(11) R.P.M. (ROYAL PORCELAIN MANUFACTURERS)
      They reproduced many character steins during the late 1940s.

(12) JOSEPH MAYER, MUNCHEN

(13) J. REINEMANN, MUNCHEN

(14) M. PAUSON, MUNCHEN
      Found stamped or impressed on stein bases and/or pewter thumblifts. Stopped
      production prior to World War II. All three were located in or near Munich. They were
      believed to be shops which specialized in the decoration and sale of various types of
      steins. They did the hand painting, affixed customized pewter lids, and, in all
      probability, did NOT manufacture the steins.

(15) GES. GESCHUTZT (also GESCHUTZ; GESETZLICH GESCHUTZ)
      Means Protected by Law; Patented; Copyrighted.

(16)   VILLEROY & BOCH
       At Mettlach. From 1841 to present.

(16a) Mercury   (16b) Castle

(17)   CAPO-di-MONTE of Ginori, Italy

(18)   REINHOLD HANKE of Höhr-Genzhausen

(19)   DÜMLER & BREIDEN
       From Höhr-Grenzhausen. 1883 to present. Stopped producing steins in 1957.

BEARS

Fig. 1

BERLIN BEAR. 1/2 liter porcelain. 8'' (20.3 cm).

The crest the bear is holding reads: "Berliner Gewerbe Ausstellung 1896" (Berlin Industrial Exhibition, 1896). The bear is colored the usual beige-brown found on many steins with the MUSTERSCHUTZ (10) mark.

SITTING BEAR. 1/2 liter pottery. 8¼'' (21 cm).

This gray, black, and brown bear holds a medallion symbolic of Berlin in its paws. The inscription along the base reads: "Xtes Deutsches Bundesschiessen Berlin 1890" (10th German Federal Republic Shooting Meet, 1890).

The REINHOLD MERKELBACH (5a) mark is incised on the bottom. Also the mold No. 734.

Fig. 2

Fig. 3

BOARS. 1/2 liter. Both steins 7¼'' (18.4 cm).

Two versions of the same boar's head. Both have extremely fine detailing. The green Tyrolean hats have various game birds' feathers. Both boars are smoking silver-lidded meerschaum pipes.

The plain pewter thumblift affixes directly to the porcelain lid. The lid consists of hat, ears, and part of the top of the head. The handle is a branch of a tree. The coloring of one boar is streaked gray, the hat medium olive green, the cord and tassle dark green. The fur of the other is a grayish brown. Tusks are white.

The green colored MUSTERSCHUTZ (10) and blue HASH (1) marks are found on the bottom. This HASH mark is thought to come from the Coburg area.

Fig. 4

CAT WITH HANGOVER. 1/2 liter porcelain. 8" (20.3 cm).

The cat is seen on many steins in a drunken condition. Since cats were considered creatures of the night, as were drunkards, this association has been carried over into folklore. We find many cats (and other animals) with a *Sauren Harung* (soured herring) limply hanging from their paws — a wonderful old world remedy for sobering up the next morning.

The most common cat of this size is found in the honey-beige browns associated so often with the MUSTER-SCHUTZ (10) and HASH (1a) marks.

Fig. 5

CAT WITH HANGOVER. 1/2 liter porcelain. 8" (20.3 cm).

More rare is the same stein with blue and white coloring. This same color is found in other animals (see Pigs). The blue is heavy at the paws, nose, and ears.

Fig. 6

CAT WITH HANGOVER. 1/2 liter porcelain. 8½" (21.5 cm).

This miserable feline is really nursing a good one. His head is bandaged, as is his aching stomach. A pillow is tucked into the bandage to support his herring. The stein is gray to match his feelings. The only coloring is in the red mouth and the red striped pillow. Tomorrow will be a better day.

NO MARKS.

Fig. 7

CAT WITH FISH. 1/2 liter pottery. 9" (23 cm).

Here our drunken friend has a few words of wisdom to the drinker: "Wer heut ist **voll** ist morgen noll" (He who is drunk today is nothing tomorrow).

NO MARKS, only MADE IN GERMANY H. T. No. 17.

Fig. 8

Fig. 9

YOWLING CAT ON BOOK. 1/2 liter porcelain. 6½" (15.8 cm) to the top of his arched back.

This grey feline is perched atop a book very familiar to students of old Germany, *The Commersbuch.* Inscribed in black lettering along the side of the beige and white book is the famous academic student drinking song of the 13th century *Gaudeamus igitur, juvenes dum sumus* (Latin: Let us therefore rejoice, while we are still young . . . soon the soil will have us). The famous composer Brahms used this passage in his *Academic Festival Overture. The Commersbuch* is found under many skull steins as well. Here the angry cat depicts the gaiety of today: be careful of tomorrow.

The pewter thumblift consists of a sausage pierced by a fork, with a radish on top. The cat has green eyes and a red mouth.

NO MARKS.

CAT. 1/16 liter stoneware. 4" (10 cm).

This tiny feline is a cobalt blue color, which brings out the details of the pebbly salt glaze finish. A manganese (violet) glaze colors the cap sitting atop his head. The cat holds a stein with the brewers' paragraph 11 on its side. The tail loops upward to form the handle.

Marked SIMON PETER GERZ (8), mold No. 030 GES. GESCH. GERMANY.

Fig. 10

Fig. 11

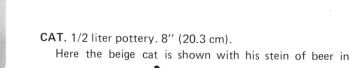

CAT. 1/2 liter pottery. 8" (20.3 cm).

Here the beige cat is shown with his stein of beer in hand, the familiar 11 is inscribed on the outside of the stein (paragraph 11 of the beer brewers' code). His nose has a hole running through it with straw whiskers inserted.

GERZ (8) marking with mold No. 061 and GES. GESCH.

18

MAMA CAT AND KITTENS. Mama cat: 2 liter; 15" (28.1 cm). Middle cat: 1/2 liter; 7" (17.7 cm). Small cat: 1/4 liter; 6" (15 cm).

The exceptionally large mother is carrying a baby kitten in a gray blanket in her right paw. The handle is in the form of a snake with its head on the bottom.

The middle-sized cat is the same color as the other two: varying shades of yellows, browns, and beiges.

The smallest cat also has a baby cat in a gray blanket in its paws.

All marked D.R.G.M. (3) GERMANY No. 154927. Mold marks: 2 liter, 736; 1/2 liter, 701 B; 1 /4 liter, 737.

Fig. 12

SITTING CAT. 1/2 liter pottery. 8" (20.3 cm).

Our drunken cat has a letter clenched in her left paw. The inscribed scroll tells her tale of woe: "Hast du Kater nimm den Rath Trinke früh was du trankst spat" (If you have a hangover take my advice. Drink early what you drank last night). The cat is sitting on its hind legs holding a smaller beige dog in her right paw. A white, untied collar is wrapped around her bottom. A red bow tie is twisted around her neck.

The figurine is colored in various shades of beige and grey. The tail forms the handle (with a bow on the end).

NO MARKS, mold No. 767.   Fig. 13

KITTY. 1/4 liter pottery.

Here our little feline friend is robed and evidently working in the kitchen, as shown by the bowl tucked under her right paw and the kitchen utensils under her left. Colors are varying shades of cream and brown.

NO MARKS, only number 774.

Fig. 14

CAT. 1/2 liter pottery. 8½" (21.5 cm).

This miserable cat is bemoaning the night before. As indicated by the scroll tucked between her hind legs: "Der Kater Laut Erfahrung Stirbt am sauren Harung" (The tomcat — hangover — according to experience, goes away with soured herring).

Colors are brown, black, and white. Again the tail forms the handle.

NO MARKS, mold No. 1000 Gesetzlich Geschutzt (15).

Fig. 15

CAT. 1/2 liter pottery. 9¾" (24.8 cm).

This large cat finally has a good solution. She is holding a bottle of seltzer in her right paw. The inscription along the base reads: "LASS Deinem Durste freien Lauf — Bei mir Kommt Kein 2ter Kater auf," which loosely translates: Let your thirst run free, with me there isn't a second hangover.

Colors are brown, grey and black.

Made by REINHOLD MERKELBACH (5a) with the mold No. 576 incised in the bottom.

Fig. 16

Fig. 17

PUSS-IN-BOOTS. 1/2 liter pottery. 10″ (25.4 cm) long, 8″ (20.3 cm) high.

This most unusual stein has many interesting details. Poking out of the brown boot are the head and paws of a mottled gray cat. The cat's escape is prevented by a secure green shoelace and a padlock on the right side of the boot. The object of the cat's gaze is a tiny gray mouse sitting at the tip of the boot. Curving behind the boot, the cat's tail provides the perfect handle.

When the pewter thumblift is depressed, the entire head of the incarcerated feline lifts upward. The stein is nearly as long as high.

NO MARKS, only No. 915 GERMANY incised.

21

SITTING DOG. 1/2 liter pottery. 8'' (20.3 cm).

This dark brown little fellow wearing eyeglasses is named Mops. The cream colored scroll reads: "Mops was kannst du nützen wenn du nicht gerollt bist" (Mops, what good are you if you are not rolled). This refers to the custom of eating *Rollmops* (rolled herring) for a hangover.

NO MARKS.

Fig. 18

SHAGGY DOG. 1/2 liter pottery. 8'' (20.3 cm).

This plain dog has a black collar encircling his neck. Tail forms the handle.

Made by SIMON GERZ (8). Mold No. 872 incised on bottom.

Fig. 19

Fig. 20

GENTLEMAN DOG. 1/2 liter porcelain. 6½'' (16.5 cm).

He wears a green hat with a dark feather. His gold-rim glasses sit on his dark brown nose. His eyes have beautiful detail.

The handle consists of a tree limb with acorns along the bottom.

Marked MUSTERSCHUTZ (10).

GENTLEMAN DOG. 1/2 liter pottery. 8½" (21.5 cm).

Wearing an olive-green Tyrolean hat, this dog has a red and gray bottle tucked under his right paw. A gun is slung over his left shoulder, with gloves in his left paw. In front of his green and olive coat is a cream colored scroll inscribed, "Wer nicht austrinkt bis auf den Grund der ist ein rechter Lumpenhund" (Who doesn't drink down to the bottom is a scoundrel tramp dog).

NO MARKS, mold No. 768 incised.

Fig. 21

BULLDOG. 1/2 liter pottery. 5" (12.7 cm).

This light beige dog has *PROSIT* incised into the banner under his paws.

NO MARKS. Mold No. 1390.

Fig. 22

Fig. 23

PUG DOG. 1/2 liter porcelain. 7½" (19 cm).

This mournful hound, with his brown and cream colored head, is one of three Character Steins manufactured by **VILLEROY & BOCH.** The others are illustrated under Owls and Monkeys.

The METTLACH castle mark (16b) and mold No. 2018 are incised on the bottom.

ELEPHANTS

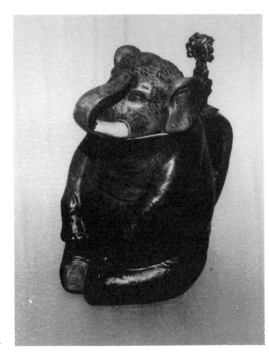

ELEPHANT. 1/2 liter pottery. 6½″ (16.5 cm).
This gray and black elephant has beige tusks.
NO MARKS. Mold mark No. 1447.

Fig. 24

ELEPHANTS. 1/2 liter porcelain, 7¼″ (18.4 cm); 1/4 liter
porcelain, 6½″ (16.5 cm).

These elephants are sitting on their hind legs with their
heads thrown back and their mouths open. The grayish
green elephant has a white stomach. The handle is formed
by the tail, at the bottom of which is a tiny, sad radish stein
lying on end.

Marked MUSTERSCHUTZ (10).

Fig. 25   Fig. 26

GENTLEMAN FOX. 1/2 liter pottery. 7½'' (19 cm).

This nattily attired fox is primarily in beiges and browns. The piping of his vest, coat, and cuffs is in blue. A blue crest appears at the base with the face of a rabbit peeping over. Certainly a tasty morsel for a hungry fox.

NO MARKS, mold No. 806. Identified in the MARZI & REMI (9) catalog.

Fig. 27

GENTLEMAN FOX. 1/2 liter pottery. 7½'' (19 cm).

This animal is holding eyeglasses in his right paw, a Bavarian grandfather's pipe in his left. A watch fob is dangling from his beige vest. A blue sash runs across his gray shirt. This fox is basically beige in color. However, he has been seen in blue-gray coloring also.

NO MARKS, mold No. 54.

Fig. 28

GENTLEMAN FOX. 1/2 liter pottery. 7½'' (19 cm).

Here our gentleman is attired in a robe. With his stein of beer and pipe, he is dreaming of conquests tomorrow. The head is brown and gray, Body a blue salt glaze.

NO MARKINGS.

Fig. 30

Fig. 29

HERR FOX. 1/2 liter pottery. 7¼'' (18.4 cm).

This fox has the same base as the Colored Duelist (see Figurals). This very colorful stein has a black coat and a brown base. His red, white, and blue sash crosses a white shirt. His brown and white face is topped by a small red cap.

Lithophane of a man smoking his alpine pipe.

NO MARKS.

Fig. 31

Fig. 32

FOX. 2 liter large master stein. 14½'' (36.8 cm).

This pouring stein is certainly one of the largest Character Steins. His head, which forms the lid, is a ruddy rust color. The body consists of varying shades of beige, tan, and brown. In his right paw is a large Bavarian pipe. Resting in his left paw -- what else? A glass of beer.

The handle is formed of two snakes, one swallowing the other.

Marked DRGM 154927 (3) Mold No. 738 Ges. Gesch. GER.

GENTLEMAN FOX. 1/2 liter porcelain. 8½'' (21.5 cm) to the top of his feather.

Under a Tyrolean hat, this fox's beige and brown face is encircled by the green collar on his coat.

The handle is a tree trunk with leaves and fruit on its back.

MUSTERSCHUTZ (10).

SAD MONKEY. 1/2 liter porcelain. 5½'' (14 cm).

Oh, such a mournful look on his face! This character is porcelain at its finest. The detail on this stein accentuates the forlorn gaze.

Coloring is the usual beige/browns associated with MUSTERSCHUTZ. However, this rare version has the mark of SCHIERHOLZ & SOHN (1b). The wording CONTROLL MUSTER also appears in black glazed script on the bottom. This refers to a sample model.

Fig. 33

MONKEY. 1/2 liter pottery. 6½'' (16.5 cm).

This comical monkey reminds one of the organ grinder's monkey of the past. He is wearing a white collar, has a brown face, bushy eyebrows, and red lips. The lid is pewter with a pottery inlay representing the top of the monkey's head.

NO MARKS, only GES. GESCH. GERMANY No. 669.

Fig. 34

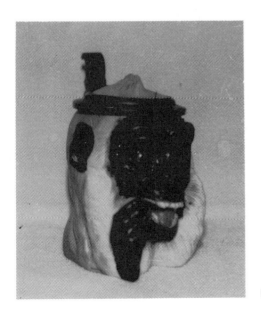

MONKEY. 3/10 liter bisque. 4½'' (12 cm).

This primate is placing a small fruit into his opened mouth. His coloring is very lifelike in its grays and whites.

NO MARKS, only M. PAUSON on the pewter thumblift.

Fig. 35

INEBRIATED MONKEY. 1/2 liter pottery. 9" (22.5 cm).

This fellow is attempting to strum a guitar. His glazed expression and his crushed hat are indications of how far gone he is. The body of the monkey is a deep brown, the hat is black, and the guitar is gold. A band beneath the verse is of a matching color to the guitar. The German verse reads: "Besitzest du solchen Affen, so macht Kein Andrer dir zu schaffen" (Once you reach this state of drunkenness — monkey on your back — you can't get any drunker).

NO MARKS, only mold No. 661.

Fig. 36

DRUNKEN MONKEY. 1/2 liter pottery. 9" (22.5 cm).

Posed in the same manner and wearing a similar crushed hat as the preceeding stein, this drunken monkey has a *Hofbrauhaus* brewery mug sitting before him. Radishes are tucked in behind the HB mug. The same German verse encircles the base of the stein. The hat and mug are tan, while the monkey's body is in varying tones of light brown.

This stein was manufactured by REINHOLD MERKEL-BACH (5a) and has the number 576 impressed in the bottom of the stein.

Fig. 37

INTOXICATED MONKEY. 1 liter. 10¾" (27.3 cm).

This beer-drenched monkey is in such a bad state that he is coming home in the mug from which he drank! His left paw holds his reeling head, and the other paw grips a dead fish (the German cure for a hangover). The red HB on the gray stoneware body stands for the *Hofbrauhaus,* Munich's largest beer hall. Two slightly different heads appear on this stein: one head is brightly colored with the eyes and mouth slightly open; the other has more subdued colors (brown tones) and the eyes and mouth are shut. Both heads have large canine teeth which protrude over the bottom lip. On some of the vessels, a glass eye is used on the fish.

NO MARKS, except GERMANY and mold No. 1286.

Fig. 38

DRUNKEN MONKEY. 1/2 liter porcelain. 7¼″ (18.4 cm).

From the looks of this slack-jawed monkey, it is quite apparent he has emptied his stein too many times. The lid of the stein in his paws is silver lustered. The primate's long tail loops to form a handle and wraps around his left side. A light brown belt circles the belly of the predominantly honey-colored monkey.

A very well done porcelain reproduction of this stein was manufactured by R.P.M. (11) in the late 1940s.

Marked MUSTERSCHUTZ (10) in glaze on the bottom of the stein.

Fig. 39

Fig. 40

DRUNKEN MONKEY, 1/2 liter 8″ (20.3 cm) tall. This stein is almost identical to the preceding monkey. The color scheme of this stein shows the white porcelain dappled with blue spots. All the body extremities (feet, hands, eyes, tail, ears and snout) are also blue. Unlike the English meaning of being "blue", the German meaning implies a state of intoxication. From the number of blue spots on our monkey friend it looks as though he is indeed, "pickled". Minute differences in detail indicate that this stein was not crafted from the mold used for the preceding monkey. Marked MUSTERSCHUTZ (10).

MONKEY. 1/2 liter. 1/2 liter porcelain. 8½″ (21.5 cm).

This monkey was manufactured by Villeroy and Boch. Mettlach produced three true Character Steins: an owl, a pug dog, and the monkey. It is generally believed that, of the three, the monkey is the scarcest. The other steins are illustrated under Dogs and Owls.

This monkey has a russet colored body with a light tan underside. His snout is also light tan. Clutched in his right front paw is a highly-glazed amber-colored fish. The presence of the monkey character on so many beer steins is attributed to an old German saying, that if you were drunk you had a monkey on your back.

The base of this stein is impressed with the V&B castle mark (16b) and mold No. 2069.

Fig. 41

29

SITTING MONKEY. 1/2 liter pottery. 9½'' (24.1 cm).

This monkey is holding his chin with his left paw and holding a plaque in his right. The plaque has the somewhat cryptic inscription: "Wie die Raupe vom Schmetterling Stammt von Affen der Kater. Wer das Söhnchen ver meiden will, Hüte sich vor dem Vater" (No more does the caterpillar derive from the butterfly, nor the monkey — state of drunkenness — from the tomcat —hangover. He who wants to avoid the son, must beware of his father). In other words, if you don't want the result, avoid the cause.

The monkey is wearing a black top hat, while his body is finished in a brown and beige glaze.

NO MARKS, only mold No. 1261 GERMANY.

Fig. 42

SITTING MONKEY. 1/2 liter pottery. 7½'' (19 cm).

This scholarly simian is intently reading a Latin tract, as the wording on the book indicates, *De Humani corporis tabrica.* Colors of this stein are varying tones of beige, gray, black, and pink.

NO MARKS, only mold No. 1444.

Fig. 43

SITTING MONKEY. 1/2 liter pottery. 9'' (22.9 cm).

This well-dressed "Beau Brummel" looks like he's ready to step out on the town. In fact, he's checking out a gold watch in his left paw to see if he's late for a date! Our dashing fellow is wearing a brown top hat and vest, both covered with red spots. A green tie completes the ensemble. The monkey's body is colored in brown tones, while his lips and tongue are red.

Marked GERMANY DRGM 154927 GES, GESCH.

Fig. 44

SITTING MONKEY. 1/2 liter salt glaze. 8¼″ (21 cm).

The monkey's body is an unusual deep brown in color. His tail loops in the back to form a handle. This fellow is clutching a cobalt blue boot to his chest. The boot most likely symbolizes the German *stiefel* (drinking boot). Many games are played with a *stiefel* on the way to getting drunk.

NO MARKS.

Fig. 45

BARREL STEIN WITH MONKEY ON LID. 1/2 liter porcelain. 7″ (17.7 cm).

The barrel has brown glaze painted on the sides to resemble wood grain. Three raised ridges at the base and the top simulate the iron bands holding the barrel together. A pewter ring encases a porcelain insert of a brown monkey sitting on a bed of green leaves. This ring bears a personal inscription dated 1885. The porcelain bottom contains a lithophane of a pair of quarreling boys with clenched fists. The combatants are standing in a grape arbor with a small dog nearby.

NO MARKS.

Fig. 46

Fig. 47

BARREL STEIN WITH MONKEY ON LID. 1/2 liter porcelain. 7½″ (19.1 cm).

The barrel is beige in color with black bands and has a brown bung. A pewter ring holds a porcelain insert on which a brown and light gray monkey sits. In one hand he holds a grey stein complete with silver luster lid and thumblift. The other hand grasps a turnip. The handle is in the shape of a fish.

Marked MUSTERSCHUTZ (10) and has the HASH mark (1) along with the number 73 on the base.

Fig. 48

MILITARY MONKEY. 1/2 liter pottery. 8″ (20 cm).

One of the Kaiser's snappy-looking warriors is the subject of this vessel. The monkey in the Imperial German Army uniform (1880-1900 period) is holding a letter that proclaims the following: "Wie die Raupe vom Schmetterling stamt vom Affen der Kater" (Just as the caterpillar does not come from the butterfly, the monkey — state of inebriation — does not derive from the tomcat — hangover).

Under his left arm hangs a broken drum while the drumstick is clutched in his hand. His feet are holding an apple and a pipe. Completing the military garb are golden major's epaulets, a black and gold *pickelhaube*, and lots of brass-colored buttons. The military tunic that the brown-toned monkey is wearing is blue with red trim. The handle is formed by a looped tail.

NO MARKS, only mold No. 769.

SITTING PIG. 1/2 liter porcelain. 6¾" (17 cm).

Pigs are found in several sizes (predominantly 1/2 liter) and positions. Here we see one seated on his haunches with his forefeet resting on his rounded tummy. His head, which forms the lid, has a silver and brown meerschaum pipe in its mouth. The pig's body is same beige/brown coloration commonly found on the MUSTERSCHUTZ (10) steins. The tail wraps around the pewter thumblift to form the handle.

Fig. 49

BABY PIG. 1/4 liter porcelain. 5¼" (13.4 cm).

Similar in appearance to the above pig. Marked MUS-TERSCHUTZ (10) and the HASH (1).

Fig. 50

PIG IN A POKE. 1/2 liter. 5¼" (13.4 cm).

This is a humorous take off of the old adage of "buying a pig in a poke" — agreeing to something sight unseen. The gray poke has the off-white pig peeking out.

Marked No. 5399 and the mark: MP

Fig. 51

BARTENDER PIG. 1/2 liter porcelain. 8½" (21.5 cm).

This pig is carrying his two mugs of beer in his right hand, a towel draped over his left. His coloring varies from the beige of his head to the light blue of his shirt and the white of his apron and towel. In his brown pants, he is standing atop a cream-colored base.

NO MARKS.

Fig. 52

SITTING PIG. 1/2 liter pottery. 7½" (19 cm).

This pink pig, sitting on his haunches, is holding a gray scroll inscribed "Vie Schwein viel Glück!" (Plenty of pig, plenty of luck). Its tail forms the handle.

NO MARKS, only No. 1260 GERMANY embossed on the bottom.

Fig. 53

34

Fig. 54

SINGING PIG. 1/2 liter porcelain. 7¼" (18.4 cm).

Here our little friend is happy with the world and singing his heart out. His arms (forefeet) are resting, as in the prior pigs, but here his ears are extended in the air.

Marked MUSTERSCHUTZ (10).

The Singing Pig is found also with folded arms, in both the 1/2 liter size and 1/3 liter size (5 3/4" or 14.7 cm).

Fig. 55   Fig. 56

SINGING PIG STANDING ON BARREL. 1/2 liter porcelain, measuring 9" (23 cm), this pig has a barrel base used for a music box. Marked MUSTERSCHUTZ (10).

Fig. 57

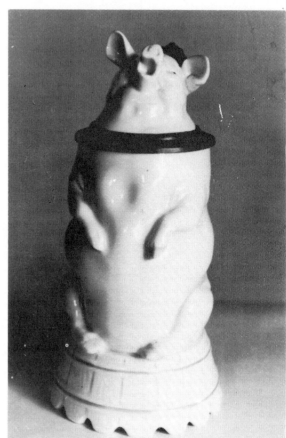

Fig. 58

PIGS. 1/2 liter. 7½" (19 cm).

These pigs are in the rarer blue and white coloring. Similar in form to the honey-colored pigs, here the snout and ears are the darker blues as seen in the ram.

Marked MUSTERSCHUTZ (10).

PIG. 1/2 liter pottery. 8½" (21 cm).

The pig's head, which forms the lid, is wearing a tan hat with a green band. In his left forefoot is a bag marked 1,000,000 (Deutsches Marks?). Several coins are falling out of his bag. His beige apron is inscribed, "Das Glück ist rund. Wer's kriegt dem ist's Gesund" (which, loosely translated, is "Fortune is around. He who gets it is in good shape"). The pig has a tan body with a blue vest and brown tie.

NO MARKS, only mold No. 770.

Fig. 59

PIG WITH CARDS. 1/2 liter pottery. 9½'' (24 cm).

This pig has ears similar to a dog's. The stein is basically beige. The scroll on the front depicts a hand holding the four suits of playing cards, with the inscription, "Zum Wohl!" (To your well being!) The base is lined in a lacy blue pattern with a brown border. The six-pointed star — possibly REINHOLD MERKELBACH (5a) — with the mold No. 1116 appearing on the bottom.

Fig. 60

PIG WITH BOWLER. 1/2 liter pottery. 9½'' (24 cm).

A similar stein is found with a scroll depicting a young lad bowling. The inscription, "Alle Neune!" (All nine) is found on many bowling pin steins (see Athletics).

Fig. 61

Fig. 62

GENTLEMAN RABBIT. 1/2 liter porcelain. 9¼'' (22.3 cm).

The hat of this rabbit is an olive Tyrolean with two beige and brown feathers tucked in to the green cord band. A monacle is in his right eye.

The stein has the varying beige/brown coloring associated with the HASH (1) and the MUSTERSCHUTZ (10) marks.

Fig. 63

Fig. 64

GENTLEMAN RABBIT. 1/2 liter porcelain. 8½'' (21.5 cm).

This rabbit is sitting in an upright position. His attire is that of the Huntsman. The jacket, complete with staghorn buttons, is strapped in the back. Across his snug-fitting vest is the leather strap of his game bag that rests on his right hip. A rifle rests under his left arm. A jaeger's hat, topped with a *gamsbart* of chamois whiskers, sits rakishly on the rabbit's head. A monacle in his right eye gives him a pompous air. The rabbit's short tail makes up the lower portion of the handle. The rest is plain.

The stein has been noted in different color schemes. Often it is seen in the beige/brown tones associated with the HASH (1) mark. It also appears with green hat and jacket. See fig. 64.

Fig. 65

SEATED RAM. 1/2 liter porcelain. 7¾ (19.7 cm).

This stein has been referred to as a goat. Close examination of the ram's horn that forms the handle indicates it is a *Bock* (ram). Coloring is predominantly a beige/brown except for the purple radishes with green leaves in the forelegs.

Marks are the HASH (1) and MUSTERSCHUTZ (10).

Fig. 66

RAM. 1/2 liter porcelain. 6'' (15.2 cm).

Similar in texture to the prior stein, this ram's head is found in the rarer blue and white coloring. The dark blue is found at the muzzle, beard, forehead, and handle, which also is formed by the horns.

Marked MUSTERSCHUTZ (10).

RAM. 1/2 liter pottery. 8'' (20.3 cm).

The ram is holding a white pipe in its right hoof and a foaming stein of beer in its left. A scroll appearing like an apron is tied on the front with the inscription: "Stösst dich der Bock Dann trotze du Wirft er dich um Dann gute Ruh!" (When the *Bock* beer or ram hits you, resist; if it throws you, then have a good rest). The stein is colored in various shades of brown and beige.

NO MARKS, just GERMANY (incised).

Fig. 67

RAM. 1/2 liter earthenware 8¾'' (22.2 cm).

If ever the *bock* had a monkey on his back, it is seen in this humorous stein. This unique stein is laden with gray HB steins, from the large earrings dangling from his ears to the many steins littered at his feet. Under his forelegs can be seen a sly fox (with a frothy stein in his hand) slinking through the mass of steins.

Coloring of this stein varies from a wooden brown in the barrel to the reds of the monkey's hat and the ram's ears. Two gray panels under his arms read: "Stösst Dich der Bock dann trotze Du" (If the *Bock* rams you, then put up resistance) and "Wirft er dich um, Dann-gute Ruh!" (If he throws you, then rest well!)

NO MARKS, only mold No. 11283 MADE IN GERMANY.

Fig. 68

RAM. 1/2 liter pottery. 7" (17.7 cm).

This ram's head and forelegs are coming out of the barrel. The scroll on the front has the same inscription as the previous one. The colors of this stein are varying browns, beiges, pinks, and gray.

Marks: D.R.G.M. 154927 (3), also mold No. 700, GERMANY Gesetlich Geschutz (15).

Fig. 69

Fig. 70

SITTING RAM. 1/2 liter stoneware. 7½" (19 cm).

This blue and gray salt glaze *Bock* shows the blue six-pointed star that is seen on many steins. It is a sign of the old Beer Measure or Indicator. The gray shield is inscribed, "Wenn man beim Bock sitzt dann schweigen alle Sorgen" (When one is drinking beer, all your cares are quieted).

Marked: MERKELBACH & WICK (4a).

41

WOLF. 1/2 liter. 7″ (17.7 cm).

His helmet appears to be an enlisted *kurassier* pattern of 1889. It has the distinctive oval base plate on the spike and the rounded front visor of the 1889 pattern. This stein could be a regimental mascot and was made as a limited production for some members of a regiment who had a wolf. German regiments had all sorts of mascots. There were even dogs who had NCO rank.

Coloring is beige and browns of the mark MUSTER-SCHUTZ (10).

Fig. 71

Fig. 72

Fig. 73

SITTING RHINOCEROS. 1/2 liter pottery. 8½″ (21.5 cm).

Colors of this mammal are grays, browns, greens, and white. A scroll inscribed *Jugend* (Youth) is held in its right hoof.

Marked with the HASH (1) mark and MUS-TERSCHUTZ (10).

RHINOCEROS. 1/2 liter pottery. 8½″ (21.5 cm).

This sitting rhinoceros is black with a mot-tled texture to show its tough skin.

NO MARKS, mold No. 1451 GERMANY.

Fig. 74

BISON. Bisque. 1/2 liter, 6" (15.2 cm); 1/3 liter, 4½" (11.5 cm).

This larger head has the fine detail often found in porcelain steins marked E. BOHNE SOEHNE (2a). Its fur is a pitch black, with a brownish face and white horns.

His smaller mate has a lock of the black fur with two horns lying atop.

STAG. 1/2 liter. 9¼" (23.5 cm) to the tip of the antlers.

This stein duplicates the actual coloring of the animal. The handle is a branch of a tree.

Marked MUSTERSCHUTZ (10) and the HASH (1).

Fig. 76

LION. 1/2 liter bisque. 5½" (14 cm).

His colors are reddish brown for the mane with a beige muzzle. The hair of the mane forms the handle.

NO MARKS.   Fig. 75

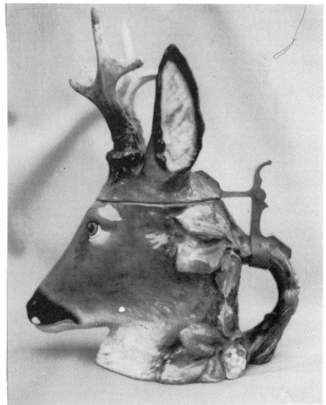

43

ATHLETICS

BOWLING

The arrangement of pins seen on the various steins is of the old German nine-pin game of *Kegelspiel*. In this game nine pins were set in a diamond shape. In the United States, old Blue Laws prohibited early Americans from playing nine-pins. The wily American colonials added a pin to get around the law and thus developed bowling as we know it today.

Fig. 77

BOWLING BALL. 1/2 liter porcelain. 5½'' (14 cm).

Of all the many steins depicting sporting events, without doubt the most common are those showing bowling or kegling.

This white stein has two pins lying on the lid. The black and red shield is inscribed with the bowlers' motto, "Gut Holz!" (Good wood). Scattered wooden-colored pins ring the sides.

Marked and No. 34.

Fig. 78

BOWLING BALL. 1/2 liter porcelain. 4½'' (11.5 cm).

This glazed wooden-colored stein is embellished with a picture of a good hit. The beige pins and ball are once again scattered over the front of the stein. The thumblift is a porcelain ball.

Marked MUSTERSCHUTZ (10).

BOWLING PIN. 1/2 liter porcelain. 8¾'' (22.2 cm).

Similar in texture, worksmanship, and coloring to the prior bowling ball stein, here we see a perfect bowling pin shape with a young boy who has jumped up on a post to avoid the flying pins of a kegler's "strike". This total scene is done in relief. The ceramic thumblift again is in the form of a ball. The top of the bowling pin is set in a pewter ring forming the lid of the stein. The stein has been noted in honey colors and dark wooden colors.

An unusual feature is that the lithophane is exactly the same scene as depicted on the front.

Marked MUSTERSCHUTZ (10) and the HASH (1) mark. Also Germany 41.

Fig. 79

BOWLING PIN. 1/2 liter pottery. 10½'' (26.7 cm).

Similar in appearance to the previous stein. Here the relief pin setter holds a scroll in his right hand which reads. "Alle Neun!" (All nine). The stein is colored a brown wood-grain. The young boy is colorfully attired in blue pants and a green jacket. His skin tones are pinkish, and he has brown hair.

Two panels on the side are inscribed: "Darfst du hurra schrein!" (You cry out hooray) and "Triffst du alle Neun" (You hit all nine).

NO MARKS, only mold No. 1140 GERMANY.

Fig. 80

Fig. 82

BOWLING PIN. 2 liter pottery. 13″ (33 cm).

A master stein. This large bowling pin has a similar relief scene as the previous two. Here the pinboy is sitting on a sling behind the scattered pins, holding the bowling ball in his right hand. Coloring is brown wood grain with beige relief. The unique thumblift is a pewter man holding a bowling ball in his right hand.

NO MARKS, only mold No. 1186 and Germany.

Fig. 81

BOWLING PIN. 1/2 liter pottery. 9½″ (24.1 cm).

This stein shows the pinboy astride a boar, with the topsy-turvy pins flying below his bare feet. The pink banner behind his head reads, ''Keglers Glück u. Stolz glatte Bahn gut Holz'' (Bowler's luck and pride-slick alley, good wood). The blue banner below him says ''Alle Neun!'' (All nine). The coloring of the body of the stein is once again a brown wood-grain.

NO MARKS, only mold No. 11132 Germany.

Fig. 83

Fig. 84   Fig. 85   Fig. 86

BOWLING PINS. 1/2 liter pottery. 8½'' (21.5 cm).

Different variations of the same pins have been noted. Here are three steins of the same size with the same mold No. 1134 Germany, but slightly different scenes. Colors vary in shades of brown.

BOWLING PIN. 1 liter porcelain. 11½'' (28.1 cm).

A unique cream-colored pin with a relief of cupid riding a pig. "Gut Holz!" is written in black lettering. The handle shows a boy holding his left hand to his chin. His right hand supports his leg. All the coloring in this stein is in the handle, with a red jacket, lavender pants, and black shoes.

NO MARKS.

Fig. 87

47

Fig. 88

Fig. 89

BOWLING. Pottery, 1 liter, 8¾" (22.2 cm); 1/2 liter, 7½" (19 cm).

The larger stein has ten wood-grained relief bowling pins or kegels surrounding the blue body of the stein. The copper-colored lid appears to be a bowling ball. The handle is a grooved ball return, with a small ball at the base.

The same stein is shown in a 1/2 liter size. The handle of this stein is a vine with a duckbill thumblift.

The 1 liter has NO MARKS, only the mold No. 1663 and GERMANY. The 1/2 liter is also marked 1663 with the THEWALT (7a) Mark.

BOWLING PIN. 1/2 liter porcelain. 7" (17.7 cm).

A plain light beige stein, with a bowling ball porcelain thumblift.

This stein is marked MUSTERSCHUTZ (10).

Fig. 90

Fig. 91

Fig. 92

Fig. 93

BOWLING PIN. 1/2 liter pottery. 9'' (23 cm).
Shows three oval panels with different men bowling. Banner on lid reads *Prosit.* Colors are a light brown wood-grain, blue banner, and multi-colored bowling figures.
NO MARKS, only No. 885 and Geschutz.

BOWLING. 1 liter pottery. 10¼″ (26 cm).

Similar to the previous steins. This kegling stein once again has the ten wood-grained pins encircling the green stein. The pins are a beige color, which matches the bowling ball lid. The lid is inscribed "Gut Holz!" (Good wood). Along the base of the lid, we read: "Das Edle Kegelspiel gibt Freuden viel" (The noble bowling game gives much joy).

NO MARKS. Mold No. 1266 Germany.

Fig. 94

BOWLING. 1/2 liter earthenware. 9″ (22.7 cm).

Nine smaller bowling pins surround one large king-size pin. Incised wavy lines account for the wood-grain texture. A filigreed thumblift connects the top of the lid (tops of the pins) to a plain handle. The following legend is found on the band at the bottom: "Lieb und Seele macht sie frei, Lustig is die Kegelei" (Body and soul make one free; happiness is bowling).

The wood grain is a brown glaze on a cream-colored earthenware body. The background and the lettering are black.

NO MARKS, only mold No. 1139 Germany.

Fig. 95

Fig. 96

FOOTBALL. 2 liter porcelain pouring pitcher with four matched 1/2 liter drinking steins. Pitcher, 12" (30.5 cm); steins, 6½" (16.5 cm).

The large orange beige stein is incised to depict brown seams. White raised lacing gives the feeling of a pigskin. It sits atop a black base.

The smaller steins are similar in color. They have red and blue pennants with U of P (University of Pennsylvania) in gold lettering. The pewter thumblifts are topped by an old-time football player's head.

Marked T. MADDOCKS SONS CO. TRENTON, N.J. DESIGN PAT. 37297 JAN. 24-05.

Fig. 97

Fig. 98

Fig. 99

FOOTBALL. Porcelain. 2 liter master stein with a set of five 1/2 liter matching drinking steins. Master stein, 12″ (30.5 cm); drinking steins, 6½″ (16.5 cm).

This beige set comes with matching pewter thumblifts in the form of the head and helmet of a football player. The following universities are represented: Columbia; Yale; Pennsylvania; Harvard; and Princeton.

Market T. MADDOCKS SONS CO., TRENTON, N. J. DESIGN PAT. 37297 JAN 24-05.

Fig. 100

Fig. 101

Fig. 102

Fig. 103

Fig. 104

Fig. 105

Fig. 106

FOOTBALL. 1/2 liter porcelain. 6½'' (16.5 cm).

Same as prior steins, but different shaped banners marked Knox, Yale, and Columbia.

Marked T. MADDOCKS SONS CO. TRENTON, N. J. DESIGN PAT. 37297 JAN 24-05.

Fig. 107

54

FOOTBALL. 1/2 liter pottery. 6¼'' (15.8 cm).

The tan pigskin with incised seams has white, slightly raised laces. To the right of the laces is a red pennant with the black letters. U.C. (University of Cornell?) incised on it. The pigskin sits on a stylized black base. The black plain handle is attached in such a way that the major features of the stein (laces and pennant) are at the stein's side.

NO MARKS only GERMANY 6.

Fig. 108

FOOTBALL. 1/2 liter pottery. 6¼'' (15.8 cm).

This glazed, cream stein is very similar to the one above. Here the seams are brown with a red pennant marked H (Harvard?).

NO MARKS, only GERMANY.

Fig. 109

FOOTBALL. 1/2 liter pottery. 6¼'' (15.8 cm).

This stein is similar to the other two, but it shows four red pennants. Coloring of the pigskin is an orange brown.

NO MARKS, only GERMANY.

Fig. 110

BARBELL. 1 liter stoneware. 10″ (25.4 cm).

Decorated with cream-colored barbells and the banner "Kraft Heil" (Hail to strength). The unusual stoneware lid depicts the ring of a weight used by a weightlifter (see next stein). The squared-off handle has relief barbells along its side. It is connected with a pewter hinge and filigreed thumblift. The body of the stein is dark green, with the barbells slightly reliefed.

The lower maroon band has the following text: "Im Herzen den Mut, im Arme die Kraft, im Humpen den edlen Gerstensaft" (In the heart, courage; in the arm, strength; in the stein, the noble barley juice).

The top band along the lid reads: "Kühn, Kernig, Kraftvoll, Kunstvoll' (Bold; Robust; Strong; Artistic).

Two crossed barbells are incised in the lid next to the text.

NO MARKS, only mold No. 1227 and GERMANY.

Fig. 111

WEIGHTS. 1/2 liter. 7½″ (19 cm).

This weightlifter's stein appears in the shape of a 25 Kg weight. (25 kilograms equal approximately 11½ pounds.) A wreath of green and tan leaves and acorns ring the *Turnvereiner*'s 4F symbol. (Information about the 4F symbol is given in detail under Fredrich Ludwig Jahn in the Famous People section — page 70.)

On either side of the wreath, the 25 Kg amount of the weight is given. The handle of the weight makes up the lid of the stein. The design work is in low relief. The stein body is black. The 4F cross, the handle, and the 25 Kg markings are red.

On the stein body, under the top of the handle, are the markings GES, GESCHÜTZT and the mold No. 1251. On the bottom, there are NO MARKS, only No. 1251 GERMANY.

Fig. 112

GOLF BALL. 1/2 liter pottery. 6½'' (16.5 cm).

This gray golf ball appears to be sitting on a brick-red tee. A pewter lid forms the upper third of the ball.

NO MARKS, only mold No. 505 incised in base. This stein also has *Rmm* and *tkh* written on the bottom in black.

Fig. 113

DIE. 1/2 liter pottery. 6'' (15.2 cm).

This white glazed die has a lid upon which are an overturned cup and three dice. The body of the stein is in the shape of a very large die. The black dots along the side are two-three-four-five in numbers.

NO MARKS, only mold No. 1781.

SOCCER BALL. 1/2 liter. 5'' (12.7 cm).

The basic colors of the stein are similar to a soccer ball (beige and brown).

NO MARKS, only mold No. 1774 and GERMANY on the bottom.

Fig. 114   Fig. 115

57

Fig. 116

LAWN TENNIS. 1 liter pottery. 10'' (25.4 cm).

Lining the outside of the stein's body are five low relief brown and beige tennis rackets. Interspersed we see many beige tennis balls, which match the four large tennis balls on the lid. The background coloring of the body is a deep green.

Along the base of the lid is the inscription, "Das edle Tennisspiel bringt Freuden viel" (The noble tennis game brings much joy).

Along the lower base is the text "Tennisspiel du edler sport dich pflggen wir an jedem ort" (Tennis, you noble sport, we cultivate you wherever we go).

Craftsmanship is similar to the Barbell stein.

NO MARKS, only mold No. 1226 GERMANY.

Fig. 117

EAGLE. 1/2 liter pottery. 9″ (22.9 cm).

This salt glaze, blue gray bird has a blue beak and pink tongue appearing from its open mouth.

Marked M. Sch and CO. ULM. MUSTER GESCHÜZT. 5

EAGLE. 1/2 liter pewter. 7½″ (18.4 cm).

This young eagle is entirely pewter, except for its yellow glass eyes with black pupils.

Marked STAIN CARRANTE PUR PARIS A LA MARQUISE DE SEVIBNE.

Fig. 118

OWL. 1/2 liter. 8″ (20.3 cm).

One of three Character Steins manufactured by VIL-LEROY & BOCH. The others are shown under Dogs and Monkeys.

This night prowler is colored in dark browns and beiges. At the base is the brown inscription, "Bibite" (To drink -- of wisdom).

Marked castle mark METTLACH No. 2036 (16b).

Fig. 119

OWL WITH JESTER'S CAP. 1/2 liter porcelain. 6″ (15.2 cm).

A very lifelike depiction of wisdom. The yellow and white jester's cap is decorated with three gold bells. The handle is formed by a tassle with three similar golden bells at the top and bottom. Orange eyes with black pupils appear to be cemented to the stein.

This brownish-gray plumed night bird is marked MUSTERSCHUTZ (10) and the HASH (1) mark.

OWL. 1/2 liter bisque. 5½″ (14 cm).

This young owl has a small, yellow, hooked beak and yellow talons. Its yellowish glass eyes are surrounded by gray stiff-feathered disks and gray and white plumage.

NO MARKS.

Fig. 120

Fig. 121

OWL. 1/2 liter pottery. 7½" (18.4 cm).

This finely feathered fellow is perched on a plain gold base. His plumage blends from a deep brown yellow on the back to a brighter yellow green on the front. The eyes and the perch are a matching green. The handle is plain with the beading design in black.

NO MARKS, only mold No. 740 GERMANY incised on the bottom. This stein, and others in the series, were copyrighted by ALBERT JACOB THEWALT (7d) in 1960. Its manufacture therefore is after that date. The Thewalt Co. was still producing this series until very recently. All the designs of these "Genuine old Beer steins" are either taken from old pieces or used the old molds.

Fig. 122

OWL. 1/2 liter pottery. 8" (20.3 cm).

This bird is colored in varying shades of brown and beige.

Marked HANKE GERMANY and mold No. 666.

Fig. 123

EAGLE OWL. 2 liter pottery. 14" (35.4 cm).

This is a very large owl. The tan and brown owl is perched on a limb surrounded by green leaves. The tannish-brown handle represents a limb also. The cream pedestal base is lined with a blue design

NO MARKS, only mold No. 584 and 11.

Fig. 124

61

EAGLE OWL. 1 liter pottery. 8½'' (21.5 cm).

Similar in texture to the prior stein, this night bird is colored purple and grey. Once again its large talons rest on a perch surrounded by green leaves. The handle is in the likeness of a limb.

NO MARKS, only mold No. 922 incised. No. 5 is also noted.

Fig. 125

Fig. 126

Fig. 127

OWL. 1/2 liter pottery. 8¼'' (21 cm).

This brown and beige owl is standing on an ornate stylized pedestal.

Marked MERKELBACH & WICK (4a).

OWL. 1/2 liter pottery. 8'' (20.3 cm).

With yellowish eyes and beak, this blue gray stein is one of the few character steins marked HR. Mold No. 64.

62

Fig. 128

ROOSTER. 1/2 liter porcelain. 7 3/4" (19.7 cm).

Another finely detailed fowl, wearing a white coat embellished with a gold medal and two brown buttons. Perched on his beige beak we see gold rimmed glasses, giving his red comb and face a worldly appearance. A black ribbon dangles from his pince-nez glasses to cover his yellow feathers, a continuation of which forms into the handle.

Marks: MUSTERSCHUTZ (10) and HASH (1).

ROOSTER. 1/2 liter pottery. 8" (20.3 cm).

This beautifully detailed bird is colored in varying shades of beiges and browns. The most lifelike beak is orange brown, the wattle a deep red. Along the side is the inscription, "Der Hahn viel besser Krähen kann wenn er die Kehle feuche an!" (The rooster can crow much better when he has a moist throat).

NO MARKS.

Fig. 130

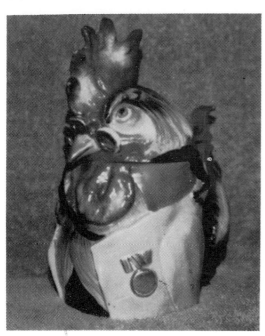

Fig. 129

ROOSTER. 1/2 liter salt glaze. 7½" (19 cm).

This chicken has a blue gray body and brownish head and feathers.

NO MARKS.

FAMOUS PEOPLE

PRINCE OTTO VON BISMARK, 1815-1898

Otto von Bismark was first named Premier and Minister for Foreign Affairs of Prussia by Kaiser Wilhelm I in 1862. Later he became Imperial Chancellor at the founding of The German Empire in 1871. He was given the title of Prince of Prussia and served his country until his resignation in 1890, during the reign of Kaiser Wilhelm II.

BISMARK. 1/2 liter porcelain. 6¾" (17 cm).

This stein depicts him in his retired civilian capacity of a country gentleman. The thumblift is, in this case, the Imperial German eagle, with the basic colors being shades of beige and brown, so common on various MUSTER-SCHUTZ (10) steins.

The base is also marked with the HASH (1) mark and the numbers 13 and 3. The 3 appears also inside the lid. This may have helped the manufacturer match the various bases and lids.

Fig. 131

BISMARK. 1/2 liter porcelain. 7'' (17.7 cm) to the top of the spike of the helmet.

Here Bismark appears in his Prussian officer's uniform and an 1867 style regular Garde helmet. Several variations of this stein are known to exist with the predominant sizes being 1/2 liter and 1/3 liter (6'' - 15 cm). This stein is normally without lithophane and comes with a variety of thumblifts. The stein body is in varying shades of beige and brown, with minor variations being noted in the dark "detail lines" on the helmet and collar.

One example has been noted in white porcelain with a blue handle, blue trim detailing, and blue floral patterns on the collar-base. These probably date from before World War I. A variation of this stein in full color is occasionally encountered in both the modern (post World War II) reproduction (R.P.M. No. 11) and the earlier Weimar Republic era (1920-1930).

Marked MUSTERSCHUTZ (10) and the HASH mark (1).

Fig. 132

Fig. 133   Fig. 134

BISMARK. 3/10 liter salt glaze. 6" (15 cm) to top of spike on helmet.

Scroll thumblift attaches to lid of stein which forms upper half of Prussian officer's "Lobstertail" helmet. The stylized helmet trappings are indicative of very high rank. The helmet plate is a Prussian eagle with the intertwined initials "FR" which stand for "Fredrick Rex" (Fredrick the Great), who was the founding father of the Prussian empire.

Oak leaves are also worked into the overall motif of the stein at either extreme of the handle and are in addition to the normal helmet fittings.

There are no manufacturer's markings on the stein. It probably dates from about the turn of the century.

Fig. 135

BISMARK RADISH. 1/2 liter porcelain. 6½" (16.5 cm).

A stylized thumblift attaches to the pewter rim of the lid, which forms the upper section of the "radish". The base of the stein is intertwined radish roots, while the body forms the face of Bismark.

Overall coloring is a grayish beige with green leaves atop the lid. Coloring and craftsmanship match the "Happy" and "Sad" radishes found in the section on Fruits and Vegetables.

The base is marked MUSTERSCHUTZ (10) small No. 9.5.

Fig. 136

Fig. 137

Fig. 138

STANDING BISMARK. 1/2 liter porcelain. 7½" (9 cm).

Here Bismark wears a *kurassier* visor cap (7th kurassiere). The white tunic appears to be a stylized artist's conception of a *kurassier koller* as worn for formal walking-out dress. He carries a court sabre in his left hand. The figure wears a Commander Iron Cross 1871 around his neck.

The lithophane depicts several tall city buildings with an onion-domed church steeple in the background.

No marks on base. The letter 'S' is incised on the thumblift with 90% on the opposite side.

BISMARK. 1/2 liter bisque. 8½" (21 cm) to tip of gold fluted spike.

The porcelain helmet depicts a helmet which was made of metal with front and neck visors, and gilt scaled chin - straps with a gilt breast eagle on front. The body of the stein is white with yellow *koller* and cuffs. The fleshtones of his face are very natural in appearance. He again carries a court dress sword with an officer's 1871 period bullion belt. His Commander's Cross is hanging from his neck.

Lithophane. NO MARKS.

Kaiser Frederich III was King of Prussia and Emperor of Germany for a very short period (March - June 1888). He married a daughter of Queen Victoria, Princess Victoria, in 1858.

FREDERICH III. 1/2 liter pottery. 7½" (19 cm) to the top of his distinctive general's dress parade *pickelhaube.*

The Kaiser wears a Commander's Cross around his neck, a Black Eagle Breast Order, and an Iron Cross ribbon in his button hole. He carries a model 1835 P guard cavalry sabre in his hand and an Order sash across his chest.

The colors are primarily a salt glaze cream with brown coat. A dark blue band lines the base.

The MERKELBACH and WICK mark (4a) is incised into the base.

Fig. 139

Fig. 140

FREDÉRICH III. 1/2 liter porcelain. 7" (17.7 cm).

As German Kaiser, he wears a General Officer's pattern spiked helmet (or *pickelhaube*). In reality this helmet would have all the gilt fittings with the Garde Star being of a matte-silver finish on the front. The center of the Star would have the Black Eagle order picked out in red, black, and green enamel. The motto "Suum Cuique" (To Each His Own) would be in gilt raised letters from the ridge of the star.

Colors of this finely detailed stein are the various shades of beige/brown associated with (1) and (10).

Frederich Ludwig Jahn was the *Turnvater* (father) of gymnastics in Germany. Jahn is most often associated with the various athletic societies throughout Germany. Their symbols were the four *Fs* in the basic shape of a cross ⌗ representing "Frish, Fromm, Froh, and Frei". This translates as "Fresh, Pious, Happy, and Free". The symbols appear on many steins (see Weightlifting).

JAHN. 1/2 liter porcelain. 6″ (15.2 cm).

The body is in the characteristic shades of beige/brown with white hair and beard. An oak leaf wreath originates from the handle and encompasses the upper side portion of the head.

Markings on the base include MUSTER-SCHUTZ (10) and the HASH (1) mark. Numbers and dates typically place this stein in the late 1800s era.

JAHN. 1 liter porcelain. 7½″ (19 cm).

Here is a variation of this stein in the 1 liter size. The color is various shades of light blue with deeper blue floral patterns lining the collar.

The same MUSTERSCHUTZ (10) mark is found on the base of this unique porcelain stein.

Fig. 141

Fig. 142

KING LUDWIG II OF BAVARIA

1/2 liter porcelain rendition of the infamous King Ludwig II of Bavaria. Measuring 7" (17.7 cm) to the top of his beige hat, this most unique stein depicts a man famous in German history. The castles of King Ludwig are the most popular sights of interest in southern Germany. Neuschwanstein Castle near Fussen (depicted on the lithophane) is kept in the style of a Knight's Castle of the Middle Ages. Born August 25, 1845 in Munich, Ludwig met an untimely death by drowning in the Starnberg Lake on June 13, 1886. The stein is in the common beige/brown tones associated with No. 1 and No. 10, but no marks were found. The edelweiss tucked into his brown hat band is yellow and white. Munich maid thumblift.

Fig. 143

UNCLE SAM. 1/2 liter. 7¼" (18.4 cm).

Colors are most frequently varying shades of beige and brown, with the face, beard, and stars in the hatband in white. A similar stein in combinations of red, white, and blue has been noted. The lid of this stein is the portion of the stein just above the hatband.

The base has the MUSTERSCHUTZ (10) marking with the HASH (1) symbol. Date markings on known examples place this in the 1900 era.

Fig. 143A

LUDWIG II. 1/2 liter pottery. 8½" (20.9 cm).

This stein shows Ludwig as he was in the mid-1870s. The artist has caught the later corpulence of the king, when his flesh became puffy and discolored. The sash is an Order sash and is normally pictured as being red in color. He carries a courtier's dress sword of the so-called "Russian" pattern.

The stein dates from the post-1871 era and was made to celebrate Bavarian patriotism in the Franco-Prussian War when, after victory over France, Germans were enthused by a feeling of being united.

No. 875 incised into base and the REINHOLD HANKE mark (18).

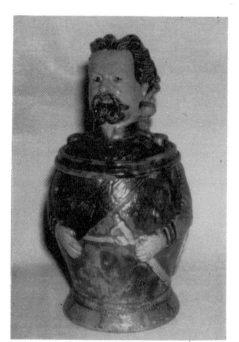

Fig. 144

COUNT HELMUTH VON MOLTKE, 1800-1891

Count Helmuth von Moltke, also known as von Moltke the Elder, was Field Marshal of the German Army during the Franco-Prussian War (1870-1871), which resulted in the formation of the modern German Empire on January 18, 1871. Wilhelm I of Prussia was proclaimed Emperor of Germany, and Field Marshal von Moltke was advanced to the post of Chief of the German General Staff, which he held until his death. (An interesting sidelight is that the nephew of the elder von Moltke was also named Helmuth and served in the same capacity as Chief of the German General Staff under Kaiser Wilhelm II at the outbreak of World War I).

Fig. 145

VON MOLTKE. 1/2 liter porcelain. 6¾'' (17 cm).

On this stein, von Moltke is wearing the off-duty officer's cap (*Offizier-mutze*), which in this case forms the lid. Von Moltke was very respected by the Kaiser and was awarded the famous "Pour le Merit", or "Blue Max", which is partially visible around his neck at the base of the stein.

Colors are variations of beige/brown with the MUSTERSCHUTZ (10) marking.

Fig. 146

VON MOLTKE. 1/2 liter pottery. 8½'' (21 cm).

This salt glaze blue and grey stein has NO MARKS, but worksmanship is similar to following stein made by MERKELBACH and WICK.

Fig. 147

VON MOLTKE. 1/2 liter salt glaze. 8½'' (21 cm).

This stein portrays the Elder in his helmet. Marked MERKELBACH & WICK (4a).

KAISER WILHELM I, 1797-1888

Wilhelm I was acclaimed King of Prussia in 1861 and Emperor of Germany following the unification of the German states at the end of the Franco-Prussian War in 1871.

Fig. 148

Fig. 149

WILHELM I. 1/2 liter porcelain. 7'' (17.7 cm).

The helmet depicted on this stein is very similar to that found on some Bismark steins, with the exception of the taller spike. The Garde Star represents the royal ''Order of the Black Eagle'' superimposed on the helmet front-plate. Characteristic features of Kaiser Wilhelm I were the ''handlebar'' mustache and large ''muttonchops''.

Colors are varying degrees of beige/brown with white mustache and sideburns. Oak leaves are also an added feature of this stein, originating from the handle and extending over the top and sides of the lid.

MUSTERSCHUTZ (10) markings on the bottom.

WILHELM I. 1/2 liter pottery. 7½'' (19 cm).

Similar in texture and size to the bust of Kaiser Frederich III. Wearing the beige dress parade *pickelhaube,* with the Garde Star imposed on the frontplate. Again the Kaiser has the Commander's Cross hanging from his neck. A black sabre is held in both his hands. Colors are generally varying shades of brown, with the cuffs, *koller* and epaulettes in black. The black order sash is incised with oak leaves.

NO MARKS. No. 13 incised in base.

Wilhelm II was King of Prussia and Emperor of Germany (1888-1918).

WILHELM II. 1/2 liter porcelain. 8¼'' (21 cm) to top of finial.

He is wearing his Garde du Corp helmet with 2'' eagle finial. This helmet is the 1889 model Kurassier, which was used until 1918. It is characterized by the sloping front visor. Wilhelm II probably did not actually wear the depicted laurels on his helmet, as these were attached to the helmets of Kaiser Wilhelm I's troops when they entered Paris in 1871. Wilhelm II was a mere 12 years old at the time.

Coloring once again is the beige/brown found with the HASH (1) and MUSTERSCHUTZ (10) marks.

Fig. 150

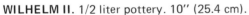

WILHELM II. 1/2 liter pottery. 10'' (25.4 cm).

Similar to the prior groupings, this beige and black stein has a *federbusch* (feather bush). The bush was made by mounting on a metal trichter or spine individual feathers, both black and white, and tying each to the trichter mount. The helmet is the same description as the general officer helmet previously described. The Kaiser holds a gala court sword of the late 1880s pattern and appears quite young. In later years Wilhelm adopted more of a curve to his moustache, and it grew more abundantly. He wears a commander's order Iron Cross of the 1871 vintage pattern. Uniform is the double breasted pattern of a general field marshal in the Prussian service. Green laurel or oak leaves incised on the order sash.

NO MARKS, No. 186 incised in base.

Fig. 151

COUNT FERDINAND VON ZEPPELIN,
1838-1917

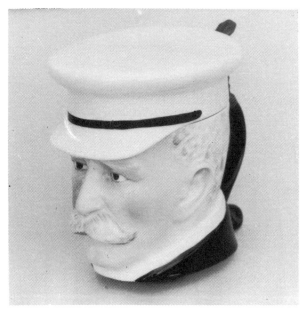

Fig. 152

ZEPPELIN. 1/2 liter porcelain. 6¼'' (15.8 cm).

His flesh-toned face has a gray mustache and brown eyes. *Graf* Zeppelin is wearing a white scarf beneath his brown collar. Germany was in a Zeppelin craze during the 1910-1912 era.

NO MARKS.

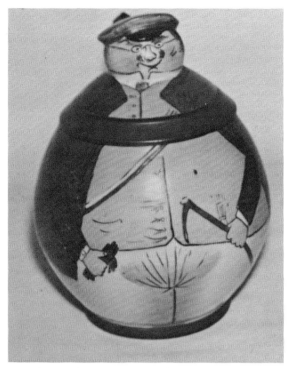

MAN (Figurals)   C-228

HOUSE (Miscellaneous)   C-440

SITTING RAM (Animals)   C-70

CHINESE MAN (Heads)   C-275

ALPINE HUNTER and ALPINE WOMAN   C-297
(Heads)

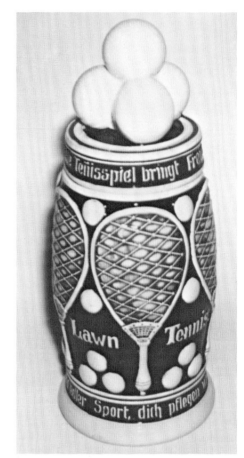

LAWN TENNIS (Athletics)   C-116

STAG (Animals)   C-76

HAPPY RADISH (Fruits and Vegetables)   C-260

ADAM AND EVE (Fruits and Vegetables)   C-252

FOOTBALL (Athletics)   C-96

TIPSY MONK (Monks and Nuns)   C-359

INSULATOR (Miscellaneous)   C-463

CHARLIE WEAVER (Figurals)   C-186

OWL (Birds)   C-121

RAM (Animals)   C-68

LADY (Figurals)   C-242

KNIGHT (Figurals)   C-250

FUNNEL MEN (Figurals)   C-196

JESTER (Jesters)   C-308

NUN (Monks and Nuns)   C-363

PAN (Heads)   C-304

SATAN (Satans and Skulls)   C-415

MONK (Monks and Nuns)   C-352

BOARS (Animals)   C-4   MUNICH CHILD (Munich Child)

INTOXICATED MONKEY (Animals) and   C-38
MUNICH CHILD (Munich Child)   C-392

MAN WITH JESTER'S HAT (Jesters)   C-311

MAMA CAT AND KITTEN (Animals)   C-12

MAID GRINDING COFFEE (Figurals)   C-176

TARGET BARREL (Miscellaneous)   C-447

TOWER (Towers)   C-416

SMILING MAN WITH JESTER'S HAT (Jester's)   C-312
RED RIDING HOOD (Figurals)   C-237

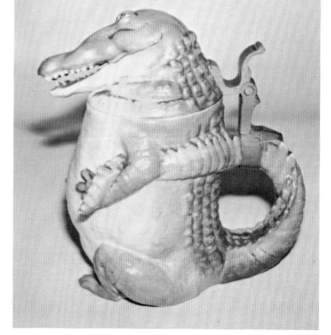

SITTING ALLIGATOR (Water Animals)   C-430

Fig. 153

Fig. 154

TIPSY CAVALIER. 1 liter porcelain. 9¾ (25 cm).

The garments of this 17th century character include the typical plumed hat and the slashed sleeves. A large leather pouch is hung from the broad belt, as is the cavalier's short sword. In his hands is a wine jug that is no doubt responsible for the glazed look of the cavalier's eyes. A plain handle and thumblift add to the stein's decorations.

This stein has been noted in two color schemes: the beige/brown of MUSTER-SCHUTZ (10) and the colored version where the lower garments are a pale green; the upper clothing yellow; the sleeve slashes are magenta, as is also the hat; the pouch and belt tan; pinkish-white plumes stick out of the hat; and the belt and sword garnished with gold leaf.

CAVALIER. 1 liter pottery. 10¾'' (27.2 cm).

This cavalier has a plumed and ribboned wide-brim soft hat in dark gray with pink band and rose-colored plume. The tunic is maroon with a pink sash. The dagger in his left hand is silver. The collar is dark cream color. The stein in his right hand is opalescent with pewter colored lid and hinge. His personal shoulder-strapped pouch is dark tan.

To the right of the handle at the base are the artist's initials. The trademark is incised on back just under point of handle attachment. No marks on bottom, only mold No. 1193.

Fig. 155

CAVALIER. 1/2 liter pottery. 7¾″ (19.7 cm).

He is holding an orange and red trumpet in his right hand. A sword is in his left. He appears to be sitting on a brown wooden stump. His green coat has a blue cape draped over the shoulders. Atop his brown hair is sitting a red hat with blue and green plumes. This stein has been seen in a blue-white salt glaze.

Marked D.R.G.M. 154927 (3). Mold No. 734.

Fig. 156

TEUTONIC WARRIOR. 1/2 liter pottery. 9″ (23 cm).

This primitive figure, with his long, flowing hair and full beard, is clothed in a belted, sleeveless shift. His head and back are covered with the skin of a brown bear. The handle is a tree trunk. He carries a horn flask in his right hand, while his left holds a shield emblazoned ''Die alten Deutschen tranken noch eins!'' (The Germanic peoples are drinking still another one). This text was taken from an old Germanic student song. It refers to the Teutonic warriors of the period from 100 to 500 A.D. Tacitus, famous historian of the Army of the Roman Legion, wrote in his report, *Germania,* of his encounters with the Germans and of their attitude of drinking ''Another one, another one''.

This stein is primarily cream-ivory in color, with the garments and features outlined in black. The shield is outlined in brown.

NO MARKS, only mold No. 1165 GERMANY.

Fig. 157

MUSHROOM MAN. 1/2 liter porcelain. 7½'' (19 cm).

The lid of this unusual stein is orange with white spots. His maroon topcoat has a dark maroon collar. The white scarf covers his ears, and a slight downturned mouth can be seen. His topcoat has four black buttons, the second from the bottom is unbuttoned. A tree branch protrudes from his back to form the handle.

Marked in the blue HASH (1) mark with the mold No. 650.

Fig. 158

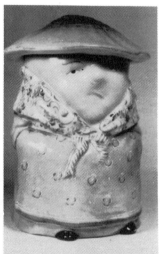

MUSHROOM LADY. 1/2 liter porcelain. 6'' (15.2 cm).

This lovely stein again has an orange mushroom for a lid. The multi-colored flowered scarf wraps around the lavender apron. Her skin-toned face has a pink nose as if she has a cold. The handle is a braid of her hair, which is tied at the bottom with a purple ribbon.

Fig. 159 Marked MUSTERSCHUTZ (10). Also No. 13. and 35.

MUSHROOM LADY. 1/2 liter. 6½'' (16.5 cm).

Here she is, holding a beige and silver stein in her right hand. Her left arm forms the handle. This lass has a lavender striped apron with a white collar and belt. Black slippers peek out from under her apron. Again she has a flesh-toned face, with a tipsy smile.

Marked MUSTERSCHUTZ (10) and the HASH (1) marks. The numbers 125 12 41.12 are incised on the bottom.

Fig. 160

79

Fig. 161

TURKISH MAN. 1/2 liter porcelain. 9" (23 cm).

The Turk's left arm forms the handle. Basic colors are the beige/browns associated with the HASH (1) and MUSTERSCHUTZ (10) marks.

It should be noted that Germany and Turkey were close from 1871 through the First World War. In 1871 Bismark invested money in the Turkish railroad system.

OLD SEA CAPTAIN. 1/2 liter porcelain. 8" (20.3 cm).

His beige coat and rain cap are offset by the tan rope which dangles over his right shoulder. The rope extends back to form the handle which is tied in a sailor's knot.

This MUSTERSCHUTZ (10) marked stein also has the HASH (1) mark and a small No. 7.58 on the bottom.

Fig. 162

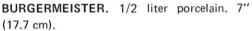
Fig. 163

Fig. 164

BURGERMEISTER. 1/2 liter porcelain. 7"
(17.7 cm).

This politician smugly has his right thumb
tucked into his tan vest. His left arm extends
behind him to hold his long white hair. It
should be noted that this stein is lacking a
pewter rim around the lid. The stein is a honey
colored combination of beiges, tans, and
browns.

Marked MUSTERSCHUTZ (10) with the
HASH (1) marks. The numbers 12. and 33 are
noted on the bottom.

SLEEPING MAN. 1/2 liter porcelain. 7" (17.7
cm).

Similar in texture and color to the prior
figure, this hunter has had a long day and is
sleeping it off. His hands are tucked into the
foxy muff. Again there is no pewter rim on this
beige and tan stein.

NO MARKS were noted on this stein.
However, from its feel and appearance, I would
classify it the same as the Burgermeister.

ALPINE MAN. 1/2 liter porcelain. 8¼" (21 cm).

A beige jacket is slung over his white shirt. The sleeve of
the jacket forms the handle. In his left hand he is holding a
brown meerschaum pipe. The basic colors of this stein are
once again beige/browns.

Marked MUSTERSCHUTZ (10) and the HASH (1)
marks. The name Pauson is incised on the pewter thumblift
with München on the other side. As so often has been
noted, the M. PAUSON (14) firm has decorated many of
these steins.

Fig. 165

81

Fig. 166

DUTCH GIRL and **DUTCH BOY.** 1/2 liter porcelain. 8½" (21.5 cm).

The girl's smiling flesh-toned face is adorned by a white Dutch hat with a wide blue band. She wears a black skirt and a green and white blouse. Her arms are casually folded over her beige and white apron.

The boy's handsome flesh-colored face has a few strands of light brown hair peeking out of his dark brown hat. He is wearing an orange red jacket with tan pants. A light green scarf is wrapped around his neck.

Marks on girl: There are no manufacturer's marks, only MUSTERSCHUTZ (10) and the mold numbers 113 and 29 embossed in the base. The small number 4 is painted on the inside of the lid and the base. This is probably the manufacturer's way of matching lid and base during production.

Marks on boy: MUSTERSCHUTZ (10) and, similar to the girl, the small number 5 is painted on the base and the lid.

Fig. 167

BARMAID. 1/2 liter porcelain. 9" (23 cm).

This buxom lass has a beige vest popping open in the front. Her white blouse is highlighted by her honey hair, which drapes behind her back to form the handle.

On the bottom are the MUSTERSCHUTZ (10) and HASH(1) marks. Also incised GERMANY 41.

Fig. 168   Fig. 169

TYROLEAN MAN and **TYROLEAN WOMAN.** 1/2 liter
porcelain. 9¾'' (24.8 cm).

The woman's lovely bisque face has blue eyes. Her hair is
blonde and her hat is olive green with a gold band and
tassle. Her scarf is dotted with pink, blue, and lavender
flowers. It is wrapped around her white blouse. A silver and
gold necklace matches the laces and buttons at her waist.

The man is similar in texture to the woman. His face has
a ruddy appearance. His hat is green with a beige feather
and gold band. He is wearing a green jacket open in front to
show his white shirt and the beige suspenders of his
Lederhosen.

These most unusual figures seem to be growing out of a
dark brown tree trunk. The trunks are lined with pink and
white edelweiss and other alpine flowers. The handles also
form tree trunks.

Both steins have lithophanes. The woman's shows the
peak of a mountain with a church and cross. The path
leading to the top has the name of the city, Wendelstein,
written on it. The man's lithophane depicts a mountainside
with two houses; Knorr Hüste is written on the path.

Marked M. PAUSON MUNCHEN 1895 (14). The num-
ber IX is written on the base of the man's stein, II on the
woman's.

83

RADISH LADY. 1/2 liter porcelain. 7½" (19 cm).

    This stein is one of a pair, the other is the Newspaper Vendor. This piece is very well done, with details so sharp that the lock of grey hair hanging over her left eye extends away from the surface. A multi-colored floral scarf covers her shoulders. Her blouse and skirt are brownish grey. The skirt is covered by a lavender-highlighted apron. In her arms she holds large white radishes with green leaves. Her head is covered by a dark blue scarf, which extends on and then separates to become the handle. The floral scarf, the face, and the hands are unusually life-like. Color is of a matte quality, making for unusual reality.

    The base of this stein is marked with the green MUSTERSCHUTZ (10) and blue HASH (1), indicative of the Coburg area of Germany. Texture is similar to quality of E. BOHNE (2), even though his mark is not apparent.

Fig. 170

NEWSPAPER VENDOR. 1/2 liter porcelain. 9" (23 cm).

    This figurine is very similar in coloring and texture to the Radish Lady. Her weathered face is realistic in appearance, even to the mole on her chin and her missing tooth. A blue kerchief and plaid shawl form the lid. The cream, rose, and brown shawl continues into the base. A newspaper is tucked into her basket.

    The MUSTERSCHUTZ (10) and HASH (1) marks appear on the bottom.

Fig. 171

BABY IN BUNTING. 1/2 liter porcelain. 8" (20.3 cm).

    This beautiful flesh-toned baby's head appears rising out of the light beige blanket. Two large purple bows are tied to this little bundle of joy. Red floral pattern is dispersed throughout the blanket.

    NO MARKS.

Fig. 172

Fig. 173

GOOSEMAN OF NURNBERG. 1/2 liter porcelain. 7¾" (19.7 cm).

This stein has the typical beige/brown coloring associated with the HASH (1) mark. The lithophane shows a view of a distant city, most probably Nurnberg. The number 205 is painted in gold leaf along the base.

Fig. 174

GOOSEMAN OF NURNBERG. 1/2 liter porcelain. 8½" (21.5 cm).

This man is similar in texture to the prior figure. However the coloring differs. His hat and coat are a deep red. A ruffled white collar appears over the pewter rim (which is lacking on the other one). His flesh-toned face supports a brown mustache and beard.

The lithophane shows a woman and two men sitting in a tavern.

NO MARKS.

Fig. 175

GOOSEMAN OF NURNBERG. 1/2 liter porcelain. 9" (23 cm).

This most ununusal stein gives the appearance of pewter, even though it is forest green porcelain.

NO MARKS, only No. 74.

The famous Gooseman of Nurnberg is depicted on many steins, not only on the stein itself, but also on thumblifts and lithophanes. The Nurnberg Trichter stein (See Miscellaneous) has a beautiful lithophane showing the Gooseman's Fountain (Der Gänsemännchen-brunnen) in front of the Nurnberg Rathaus. The fountain was cast in bronze by Pankraz Labenwolf in 1550.

MAID GRINDING COFFEE. 1/2 liter porcelain. 9-7/8'' (25 cm).

This large advertising stein portrayed a coffee of the day. Inscribed along the base is "Kathreiner's Kneippmalzkaffee" (Katherine's Children's Malt Coffee -- no caffeine).

The bisque woman is grinding the coffee in her beige mortar. On her right side is seen a bag of Katherine's Coffee, and under her left arm is a gray coffee pot. Her blue striped blouse is covered by a light beige apron, in the front of which is tucked a red rose.

This stein has been noted with a solid base marked MARTIN PAUSON, MUNCHEN (14) and with a lithophane showing the same coffee bag. Surrounding the bag is the inscription, "Gesundheit, Genuss, Ersparniss" (Health, enjoyment, thriftiness).

Fig. 176

LITHOPHANE

Fig. 177

Fig. 178   Fig. 179   Fig. 180

KATHREINER'S KNEIPP-MALZ-KAFFEE. 1/2 liter porcelain. 6½'' (16.5 cm).

This most unusual stein compliments the prior maid. This realistically colored stein portrays the bag shown in the lithophane. The bag is an off-white, and on the front panel is a blue-line rendition of Kathrein. On the side panels are the medals and inscriptions in red. A pewter thumblift adorned with a Munich maid completes this rare beauty.

NO MARKS. Only N.B.M. incised on the side of the pewter.

ELF. 1/2 liter pottery. 7½'' (19 cm).

This jolly looking, robust man is forest colored, from the olive green of his hood and jacket to the browns of the tree stump he is leaning on. His brownish beard starts on the lid and passes through the pewter rim to hang down upon his rotund stomach. A small cigar hangs from his lips. In his right hand, a bunch of gray keys hang. Yellow pants and red shoes complete this colorful character.

Marked D.R.G.M. (3) and mold No. 694. Gesetzlich geschützt and GERMANY also appear on the bottom.

Fig. 181

Fig. 182

INDIAN CHIEF. 1/2 liter porcelain. 8½″ (21.5 cm).

This colorful figure depicts a sorrowful sitting Indian. His skin-toned face is lined with blue and red war paint. In his hand is a brown peace pipe. His brown buckskin coat covers his light blue pants.

NO MARKS.

MAN. 1/2 liter bisque. 10″ (25.4 cm).

This large stein shows this fellow with a very placid look on his face. A gray flask of liquid refreshment sticks out of his right pocket. His light beige suit covers his brown vest and blue striped shirt. Red suspenders boldly hold his sagging pants up. Matching red neckerchief completes his attire for the day. His black top hat has a wide yellow band.

NO MARKS, only No. 46. The inscription in the pewter rim dates this stein as 1905.

Fig. 183

Fig. 184

SNOWMAN. 1/2 liter porcelain. 8¼″ (21 cm).

This figurine is actually a penguin holding a long stem pipe in his hands. His hat, eyes, nose, mouth, and pipe decorations are a deep blue on a bluish-white background.

Marked MUSTERSCHUTZ (10).

MONEYBAGS. 1/2 liter porcelain. 7'' (17.7 cm).

This happy fellow clutching a brown money sack (100,000 painted on the side) is content with the world. His tipped olive green hat has a white nightcap hanging out. Is he heading for the bank so early in the morning? His flesh-toned face, with ruddy cheeks, sits atop his light blue coat. A green tie, purple vest, and black slacks compliment this humorous man.

This stein is marked with the mold No. 403 and

Fig. 185

CHARLIE WEAVER. 1/2 liter soft paste porcelain. 9'' (23 cm).

This stein depicts a mustached man with a pair of glasses hanging low on his nose. In his right hand is draped a cat (a drunken cat?). he wears a crushed black high hat, which forms the lid. The body of the man is done in relief, with panels on each side of the handle. The left panel says, "Und Ich bring doch manchen Kater (nach) Haus von diesem Plätzchen" (And I bring you home indeed many hangovers from these little places). On the right panel is, "Du lockst Keine Katz hinterm Ofen raus, so sagt mein ehrich schatzchen" (You can't entice any cats out from behind an oven -- so says my honest little sweetheart).

Wearing a gray shirt, red vest, yellow brown trousers, and a light brown coat, he has light brown hair and mustache. This "Little Man" character has been depicted by many cartoonists as the symbol of an inebriate. The late Cliff Arkett possibly used this figure to develop his Charlie Weaver character.

Marked DRGM 154927 (3) and mold No. 765 are incised in the base.

Fig. 186

Fig. 187

END MAN IN A MINSTREL SHOW. 1/2 liter pottery. 7½" (19 cm).

This stein has been noted in many configurations. Some with lithophanes (monk with young woman — the woman has downcast eyes and the monk is comforting her), some with a plain base. The coloring varies also. His black face has white cuts on his right cheek (a duelist perhaps?) and a slash on the forehead and left cheek. His green hat, which forms the lid, appears with either a yellow medallion (SC initialed within), or, on some, just a plain yellow medallion with red and blue edging. The minstrel is wearing a brown coat, blue, yellow and red sash, and a large red, white, and blue checked tie. In his left hand is a long alpine pipe; his right is holding a black walking cane. The handle is in the form of a bamboo walking stick.

Incised in the base of the plain steins is the mold No. 1005 and GESCHÜTZT.

Fig. 188

BLACK MAN. 1/2 liter porcelain. 6" (15.2 cm).

This highly glazed stein is wearing a red, blue, and white jacket. His lips are a bright red to contrast with the white of his teeth and eyes.

NO MARKS, just No. 138 incised in the bottom.

Fig. 189

HEIDELBERG BLACK STUDENT. 1/2 liter porcelain. 7½" (19 cm).

This student is wearing a small red, white, and black skull cap with solid red top. His facial slashes are very similar to the previous stein. Gold earrings are also dangling from his ears. The base consists of a black coat, white shirt, gray vest, beige pants, and a gold watch chain and fob. A red, white, and blue sash crosses his chest. The base portion of the stein is exactly the same as the Fox (see Animals).

Two different lithophanes have been seen. One shows a monk and young maiden holding a loaf of bread. The other shows a monk consoling a woman. She is wearing a beautiful necklace. The monk has his arm around her shoulder.

NO MARKS.

Fig. 190

HEIDELBERG STUDENT. 1/2 liter porcelain. 9'' (23 cm).

This stern student has his marks of courage slashed on his right cheek. This highly glazed figure has a stein in his hand inscribed "Gaude Amus Igitur". His left hand is casually inserted in his green trousers' pocket. A yellow vest is crossed by the red, white, and blue sash seen in prior steins. A black suit coat, white shirt, and lavender tie complete this stein.

Marked with the HASH (1) mark.

A similar 1/2 liter stein comes in a pottery finish. Colors and size are the same, but the facial expression is much more severe than the porcelain version.

NO MARKS, only mold No. 1195.

CHINAMAN. 1/2 liter. pottery. 7¾'' (19.7 cm).

This barrel-shaped figure has been made in a variety of colors, ranging from beige/brown with black trim to colorful red and blue sleeved versions.

The six-pointed "Beer Measure" appears under each arm. The inscription on the stomach panel reads, "Mensch ärgere dich nicht" (Don't aggravate yourself).

NO MARKS.

Fig. 191

Fig. 193

Fig. 194

FUNNEL MAN. 1/2 liter pottery. 9½" (24 cm).   Fig. 192

Similar in texture and workmanship to the prior Chinaman, this barrel-shaped man has a lid in the shape of a funnel. This could associate very closely with the famous Meistersingers of Nuremberg. Many steins are pictured with the funnel as part of the decoration. The most famous of these is the Nürnberger Trichter (see Miscellaneous).

His droopy brown (sometimes red) pants match the sleeves in coloring. His cuffs, collar, and shoes are dark brown. Again the six-pointed star appears under each arm.

The stein appears with two different inscriptions on the front panel. One reads, "Mensch ärgere dich nicht" (Don't aggravate yourself), and the other "Mann ärgere deine Frau nicht" (Don't aggravate your wife).

NO MARKS, only mold No. 622. Identified in the REINHOLD-HANKE catalog.

LANDLORD, 1/2 liter, porcelain, height is 7" (17.7 cm). Attired in his lavender robe the landlord is on his rounds. Two red seals dangle from the white scroll he is carrying. The scroll is inscribed "PACHTVERTRAG VUN KIAUTS-CHAU" (Rent agreement from Kiautschau). Kiautschau was the only city in China actually rented from the Chinese for 99 years. It is called Tientsin now. The Germans trained many Chinese troops between 1880 and 1914. Under the landlord's right arm can be seen a running rabbit. Supposedly to signify someone who tries to be a bigshot. The lid consists of his stern flesh-toned face with a green oriental cap and white collar. The handle is formed by an extension of his braided hair. This stein also appears in the beige/brown coloring of Musterschutz. NO MARKS were apparent, only the signature C. Bauer, Arzberg on the base.   Fig. 195

FUNNEL MAN. 1/2 liter pottery. 9½" (24 cm).

Same stein as the prior, but appears in the blue gray salt glaze finish.

Fig. 196

MANDARIN MAN. 1/2 liter salt glaze pottery. 7" (17.7 cm).

This blue and gray figure holds his hands on his rotund stomach, very similar to the many monk and nun steins (see Monks and Nuns). The base of this stein has been used interchangeably with various lids.

NO MARKS. Mold No. 67.

Fig. 197

SMILING CHINAMAN. 1/2 liter salt glaze pottery. 7½" (19 cm).

The basic coloring of this stein is varying shades of blue and gray. The face is set off by a small oriental cap. In the 1890s, Germany acquired a concession on the Shan-Tung peninsula in China. This may account for the number of Chinese styled steins in the 1800s, as Germany increased her trade and became the second largest manufacturing country in the world by 1914.

NO MARKS.

Fig. 198

MANDARIN WOMAN. 1/2 liter salt glaze pottery. 7" (17.7 cm).

Similar to the prior figure. This lady is colored in blues and grays with purple hair. Again the base may be interchangeable with other lids.

NO MARKS.

Fig. 199

CHINAMAN. 1/2 liter pottery. 7¼" (18.4 cm).

This finely detailed character is predominantly blue and yellow in coloring. His face is very realistic, from the mustache to the teeth.

Marked MERKELBACH AND WICK (4a).

Fig. 200

RICH MAN. 1/2 liter pottery. 8" (20.3 cm).

This robust, seated gentleman is nattily attired in a speckled yellow vest, from which protrudes a yellow fob. A deep purple coat passes through the pewter rim to form the lid. Upon his white shirt, a red and white tie rests. His ring-covered fingers are tucked into his vest. Wearing green pants, his pixie-like pointed shoes rest in front. The base is red, the hat is black.

Marked THEWALT (7a) and mold No. 175.

Fig. 201

RICH MAN. 1/2 liter salt glaze pottery. 6 ½" (16.5 cm).

This affluent gentleman once again appears in the blue and gray coloring seen in the prior steins.

Marked MERKELBACH AND WICK (4a).

Fig. 202

YOUNG MAN. 1/2 liter salt glaze pottery. 7½″ (19 cm).

Colored blue, with a gray face and shirt, this lad is very casual with his hands tucked into his pockets. A small flask is tucked into his left pocket.

NO MARKS.

Fig. 203

MAN. 1/2 liter salt glaze pottery. 8½″ (21.5 cm).

This tipsy blue and gray lad is sitting atop a small keg marked "Prosit". An open stein of beer appears in his right hand.

Marked HR and mold No. 63.

Fig. 204

MAN. 1/2 liter salt glaze pottery. 7½″ (19 cm).

Basically colored blue and gray, the striped beige coat and brown alpine pipe are the only contrasting colors.

NO MARKS, only mold No. 805 is incised in the bottom.

Fig. 205

Fig. 206

Fig. 207

BEER BARREL MAN. 1/2 liter pottery. 8''
(20.3 cm).

The basic colors are browns and tans. He is
holding a beige radish in his left hand, a
dumbbell in his right. The brown hat has a
small 4-F insignia on the front to match the 4-F
on the pewter thumblift. Inscribed on the beige
band on his chest is "Gut Heil!" (Good health).
His face appears very similar to "The Great
Gildersleeve" (Harold Peary).

Marked J. REINEMANN MÜNCHEN (13).

BEER BARREL MAN. 1/2 liter salt glaze
pottery. 8'' (20.3 cm).

Similar to the other one, this commemora-
tive stein is dedicated to German athletics. It
is inscribed "Gut heil Gruss aus München VII
Deutsches Turnerfest" (Good health. Welcome
to Munich's 7th German Turner fest).

Marked J. REINEMANN MÜNCHEN (13).

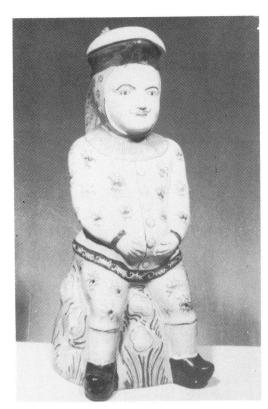

MAN. 2 liter. 13½" (34 cm).

The male figure of a pair of very singular Character Steins. The man is seated on a bank of flower-like objects. He is dressed in a regional folk costume (most likely that of the 18th century Lowlander -- a Dutchman, in other words). The man's deformed figure includes a bulging potbelly and a hunched back. The delicate features of the face, and the somewhat furrowed brow, give the man a puzzled look. His attire includes wooden shoes, knickers, a colorful white jacket (with red and blue flowers and blue trim), and a green headgear that exposes only his face. Small star-like designs cover the hood. The highly curved green handle appears mottled with purple spots. It emerges from his hunchback. A small pewter thumblatch attaches the top of his hat to the handle. The perch of this stein is green with yellow and red flowers. This type of craftsmanship is usually attributed to those products known as polychrome delft.

NO MARKS only a glazed blue No. 9 on the bottom.

Fig. 208

WOMAN. 2 liter. 13" (33 cm).

This is the female mate to the preceding stein. The woman also possesses a hunched back but lacks the protruding stomach. She sits on a similar mound. Her outfit matches that of the man and includes black wooden shoes, a light violet apron covered with red flowers, yellow dress, and a white jacket with flowers and cobalt blue trim. The starched bonnet is white with two blue slashes on either side. The hat, which lifts off with the aid of a pewter thumblift matches the flowered jacket. Her handle is green and mottled with purple. Her eyes are blue, in contrast to the man's brown eyes.

NO MARKS.

Fig. 209

WOMAN. 1/2 liter. 8½" (21.5 cm).

A smaller version of the prior two steins, this delft sitting woman is attired in a brightly colored dress speckled with red flowers with green leaves. A slight smile lights her white face. Once again her hat forms the lid for this very colorful stein.

Marked No. 171E, the worksmanship is attributed to Francis Bussart of Lille, France (ca. 1680).

Fig. 210

MAN and **WOMAN.** 1 liter salt glaze. Man, 12½" (31.7 cm); woman, 11½" (29.2 cm).

A matched pair. They are both in a textured gray. Clothing and head attire are blue. They are both sitting atop small barrels. Both heads swivel in their pewter rims.
NO MARKS.

Fig. 211   Fig. 212

MAN and **WOMAN.** 1 liter pottery. Man, 12"
(30.5 cm); woman. 11½" (27.9 cm).

Similar to the previous couple. This pair is
colored.

The man sits atop a wooden brown barrel
with gray bands. His green frock coat and gray
green britches encompass his round tummy.
The lid consists of his smiling, skin-toned face
with rosy cheeks and brown muttonchop whiskers.

The lady is sitting atop a wooden tree
stump. Her dress is blue gray with matching
bonnet. Brown hair sets off her pretty smiling
face.

Both heads swivel in their pewter rims. When
they are happy with one another, they fondly
gaze into each other's eyes. When he has drunk
a little too much, she may turn away. A very
unusual pair of figurines.

The man is marked THEWALT (7c) and
mold No. 487. The woman is marked THE-
WALT (7c) and mold No. 488.

Fig. 213   Fig. 214

RICH MOTHER-IN-LAW. 1/2 liter pottery. 9½" (24 cm).

Attired in her lovely dark blue dress, marked with a
beige floral pattern, and with her red shawl casually draped
over her arms, this beautiful woman carries a beige sack of
money (inscribed 150,000 M). Is she out to visit her family,
or going to the bank? Along the beige base is written, "Das
ist die liebste Schwiegermamama!" (This is the loving
mother-in-law). A fine tribute to in-laws the world over.

There is a false bottom in this, with provision for a
music box.

NO MARKS, only mold No. 680. Geschützt.

Fig. 215

FIREMAN. 1/2 liter salt glaze. 7" (17.7 cm).

A similar blue and gray appearance to prior salt glaze steins is found in this stein. His fireman's helmet (*Fuerwehrhelm*) is distinctive with its brass comb. No other Imperial unit took this pattern. The frontplate has crossed fire axes and what appears to be a fireman's helmet. The rope around his plump mid-section indicates fire rescue work. Firemen's uniforms differed from state to state and the devices on their helmets also differed, though the crossed axes and the helmet of brass in profile were almost always used as a belt buckle device, if not on the helmet.

NO MARKS. Ca 1889.

Fig. 216

FIREMAN. 1/2 liter pottery. 7½" (19 cm).

This stein depicts the fireman in his blue uniform, red collar, and black helmet. He is holding a beige hose in both hands, a light beige rope is wrapped around his waist with the inscription "Gut Schlauch" (Good hose). The red F, indicative of Fireman, is on his right chest.

Marked MERKELBACH AND WICK (4a). The No. 383 is incised on the back of his beige belt.

Fig. 217

MINER. 1/2 liter pottery. 9" (23 cm).

The basic coloring of this figure is varying shades of brown, beige, and black. On his shield is inscribed "Glückauf" (Come up with luck) and crossed hammer and awl. The same design appears on his cap. He appears to be sitting on a large piece of coal.

NO MARKS, only No. 736 incised on the bottom.

Fig. 218

BARMAID. 1/2 liter pottery. 10¾" (27.3 cm).

Her dress is aqua, covered with a rust colored apron. Her left hand is inserted into a brown money bag. Green leaves and red berries ring the base, which has a false bottom for a music box. Her skin-toned face, with rosy cheeks comprises the lid of the large stein.

NO MARKS, only No. 1089.

Fig. 219

NIGHT WATCHMAN. 1/2 liter pottery. 8½" (21.5 cm).

Carrying a lantern in his left hand, he holds a foaming mug of brew in his right. A weapon leans in his arm. His olive coat and cap are contrasted by a rust colored shawl. Inscribed on the mug is "Letzte Runde" (Last round -- of the night? or the beer?).

NO MARKS.

Fig. 220

FANCY LADY. 1½ liter pottery. 15¼" (38.7 cm).

Dressed in a long lavender dress with short puffed sleeves, belted with fan attached, her shoulder shawl is fringed in a variegated orange. She wears buttoned, elbow-length, gray gloves. Her long brown wavy hair extends to her waistline. Hat is black with a red plume. A beading appears at the hemline. This stein has a white scrolled handle with decorative animal heads on the top and bottom.

Marked D.R.G.M. 154927 (3) Gesetlich Geschutz. Mold No. 732.

Fig. 221

101

HOBO. 1/2 liter pottery. 8'' (20.3 cm).

Here is a most interesting character who has almost disappeared from the scene. Bald-headed, with hat in one hand, knurled twisted walking stick in the other, he is clad in purple patched trousers, brown patched jacket, blue vest, and gray shirt. An extra pair of shoes is carried on a green sling around his left shoulder. We see the "King of the Jungle" as he proudly makes his way. The perfect gentleman with a little flower in his lapel. At his feet of worn shoes are mushrooms and rocks. He sits on a stump from which a branch forms the handle. The stein is of a matte finish.

NO MARKS, only No. 723 incised. Companion to No. 724, the Jolly Fat Lady.

Fig. 222

JOLLY FAT LADY. 1/2 liter pottery. 7¼'' (18.4 cm).

Holding a stein in her right hand, this happy lass is pulling up her yellow and orchid dress to reveal her pantaloons and the mushrooms and rocks below. This colorful stein is set off by a blue apron, green scarf, purple socks and brown shoes. She appears to be sitting on a tree stump, from which the branches form the handle.

NO MARKS, only mold No. 724. Companion to No. 723, the Hobo.

Fig. 223

BARTENDER. 1/2 liter pottery. 8½'' (21.5 cm).

Sporting a brown cigar, this robust man is evidently chatting with his customers. His purple trousers are covered by a beige apron.

On the two panels on the rear are the inscriptions "Laast sie nicht vergeblich winken" (Let them not wave in vain) and "Da uns noch die Krüge winken" (If the steins do still invite us). Our loose interpretation shows the many steins sitting on the wall of the bar waving and inviting the patrons to indulge in the beer.

Marked D.R.G.M. (3) 154922 GES. GESCHUTZT GERMANY Mold No. 763 B.

Fig. 224

MAN and WOMAN. 1/2 liter pottery. 6¾'' (17 cm).

This glazed couple is very similar in coloring. The man is wearing a rounded brown hat which forms the lid. In his folded arms he holds an alpine pipe. His pink vest is covered with yellow buttons. Inside of the stein is glazed aqua. On the bottom is the following marking:

The woman has the same beige and brown coloring. Her hands overlap on her brown coat. She almost appears to have a startled look to her robust face. Same markings as above, only with mold No. 138 incised.

Fig. 225

PERKEO. 1/2 liter porcelain. 8'' (20.3 cm).

This bisque figure has a long wig dangling from his green cap. His coat, vest, and pants are a similar deep green, lined with gold trimming.

Perkeo was a dwarf·and court jester in the days of Elector Carl Phillips (1716-1742), famous to this day for his drinking powers. History indicates Perkeo became a legend of all jesters. In the Great Tun (the world-famous Heidelberg wine cask, having a capacity of 221,726 liters), is a figure of Perkeo.

NO MARKS, only mold No. 613 incised in the bottom.

Perkeo, Heidelberg's famous court jester

Fig. 227

Das grosse Heidelberger Fass, 212 422 Ltr. fassend.

104

MAN. 1/2 liter pottery. 6½" (16.5 cm).

This portly "Pinhead" gentleman must be out for a day at the races, as evidenced by his riding crop and gloves. All features are painted on this stein, from his gray cap to his redbrown coat and yellow vest.

NO MARKS.

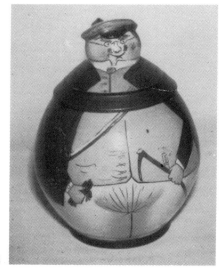

Fig. 228

BARMAID. 1/2 liter pottery. 6" (15.2 cm).

Similar in manufacture to the prior stein, this painted maid carries six mugs of beer. Her brown dress is covered by a blue apron.

NO MARKS, only mold No. 1571 Germany.

Fig. 229

ROLY-POLY SOLDIER. 1/2 liter pottery. 8" (20.3 cm).

This humorous stein has a blue-tailed jacket lined in pink. Collar, cuffs, frontispiece, and epaulets are red. Gold and white slings criss-cross his front and back. White trousers and black shoes complete the attire.

NO MARKS. Mold No. 1577 Germany.

Fig. 230

105

WOMAN. 1/2 liter glazed pottery. 8" (20.3 cm).

This smiling woman, wearing a light brown bonnet, has a blue umbrella in her hand. A wide red belt wraps around her blue dress. Standing on a beige pedestal base, this stein is similarly painted to the Roly-Poly soldier.

NO MARKS. Mold No. 1579 Germany.

Fig. 231

HUNTER. 1/2 liter pottery. 8" (20.3 cm).

In his long brown top-coat, with two dachshunds peeking out of either side, this gray-bearded gentleman is out for the hunt, as evidenced by the gun held behind his back.

NO MARKS.

Fig. 232

MAN. 1/2 liter pottery. 8" (20.3 cm).

With blue and white striped base and trousers and peaked brown hat, he wears a brown coat and a red and white checkered vest.

Marked GERZ (8) and mold No. 1305.

Fig. 233

WOMAN WITH BABY. 1/2 liter porcelain. 8½″ (21.5 cm).

This smiling lady is dressed in lavender with a beige apron. Her brown hair has a small red hat atop it. Bisque finish.

NO MARKS, only mold No. 1580 Germany.

Fig. 234

LADY. 1/2 liter salt glaze pottery. 7½″ (19 cm).

With her ruffed neck and sleeves, this lady could possible be a queen or lady in waiting. Her bulbous brown body offsets the blue grays typical of this salt glazed finish.

NO MARKS.

Fig. 235

GAMBRINUS. 1/2 liter pottery. 7½″ (19 cm).

The body of this figural is barrel-shaped, having brown staves and four cream bands. His flesh-toned face is covered with a black beard and purple crown to denote the "King of Beer".

Gambrinus was known as the patron saint of beer. He is said to have invented the beverage. A small spigot appears from the barrel.

Marked DRGM No. 154927 (3). Mold No. 705 GERMANY.

Fig. 236

Fig. 237

CHILDREN'S STEINS. 1/4 liter pottery. Sizes
vary from 5½'' (14 cm) on the left to 7'' (17.7
cm) on the right.

Children learned the taste of the hops at an
early age, as evident by the four pictured steins.
The Munich Child is described in more detail
(see Munich Child section).

All marked J. REINEMANN, MÜNCHEN
(13).

Fig. 238

GAMBRINUS. 1/2 liter pottery. 7½'' (19 cm).

A gray and blue salt glaze figure of the
''King of Beer''. Along the base of this stein is
the inscription ''Gambrinus bin ich genannt der
zuerst das Bier erfand'' (Gambrinus I am called,
who was first to invent the beer).

Marked REINHOLD MERKELBACH (5a).

IRON MAIDEN FROM NURNBERG. 1/2 liter salt glaze pottery. 8¾'' (22.2 cm).

This purple gray stein depicts a macabre instrument of torture. In days of old, a prisoner would be placed within the chamber of the ''Maiden'' and the spiked door slowly closed until the desired information was obtained.

The handle of the stein is the likeness of a heavy chain. Two hinges are on either side of the body, and the front doors are opened by the two large handles. A large chain circles the base for the locking of the doors. Heavy rivets are embossed upon this grizzly lady.

On the back of the body are two panels inscribed, ''Ich alte Nürnbergerin bracht' sonst den Tod jetzt helf' ich dirst 'gen aus der Not'' (I, the old Nürnberg gal, once brought death; now I help the thirsty quench their thirst). Along the base is the inscription ''Eiserne jungfrau zu Nürnberg'' (the Iron Maiden of Nürnberg).

Marked T. W. Gesetzlich geschutzt.

Fig. 239

Fig. 240

BAVARIA. 1 liter pottery. 11'' (28 cm).

This stein represents a very famous statue in Munich. Over the Theresienwiese, the scene of the Oktoberfest, rises the Bavaria with the Ruhmeshalle (Hall of Fame) as a gigantic symbol of the Bavarian state and Bavarian patriotic pride. The bronze statue, a gift of King Ludwig I to his people, was modeled by Ludwig Schwanthaler, cast in the Miller foundry, and unveiled during the Oktoberfest in 1850. The monument measures 20 meters, base included. An inner stairway leads upward into the head, where small windows offer a broad panorama of the city. The Ruhmeshalle (1843-53), by Klenze, constructed as a Doric columned hall in an open rectangle around the Bavaria, once contained 84 marble busts of men who had earned the esteem of the state of Bavaria. The Bavaria is found on the lithophane of many steins.

LITHOPHANE

110

WOMAN. 3 liter pottery. 11" (28 cm).

    This pretty lady is a serving stein of purple and gray salt glaze pottery.

    NO MARKS, only No. 224 incised in the bottom.

Fig. 241

LADY. 1/2 liter silver. 9" (22.9 cm).

    This rare, jeweled, coin silver stein pictures a lady. Hanging from her ears are two golden yellow earrings. On her bodice are pink and white stones. Along the base are eight additional large jewels. The lid opens at her hairline and is attached to the handle, which is formed as a continuation of her hair. To complete the decoration of this most unusual figural, we find a silver crown on the back of her head.

    Marked C2B and

Fig. 242

BEARDED MAN. 1/2 liter pewter. 8" (20.3 cm).

    Entirely crafted from pewter, this rotund figure's face is bearded with a long flowing brush that covers the frontal portion of the stein. Atop the figure's head is a pewter cap that is heavily adorned with hops and grapes, as is the base. The handle of the metal jug is fashioned in the form of a semi-nude girl. A dark, uniform patina covers the figure.

    Engraved on the stein bottom is a mark encompassing the inscription: B & G Imperial Zinn.

Fig. 243

LADY WITH BUSTLE. 1/2 liter pewter and stoneware. 9¾" (24.8 cm).

The lower body of this fashionable woman of the Gay Nineties is of blue and gray salt glaze. The details of her dress are highlighted in a rich cobalt blue. The upper portions of the woman's bustle and her torso are crafted from cast pewter. The costume of the woman is completed with a bonnet and a parasol that forms the handle. Most Character Steins face away from the handle, but this is not the case with this piece. In this instance the finial head is depressed and the bustle opens up to receive the beer.

Marked HR.

Fig. 244

LADY WITH BUSTLE. 1/2 liter pewter and stoneware. 9¾" (24.8 cm).

A similar stein to the prior one, here the pewter bustle is more finely detailed to flow into the lines of the stoneware base. The parasol she wears does not attach to the handle as above.

Marked HR.

Fig. 245

MEPHISTOPHELES TEMPTING THE MAIDEN. 1/2 liter pewter. 9½" (24 cm).

A little humor in days of yore. A similar maiden to the prior stein is being tapped on the shoulder by a smiling comical Satan. Will she be led astray?

The detail of this unusual vessel is finely done from the top of the bonnet to the spindle-legged devil.

NO MARKS.

Fig. 246

KNIGHT. 1½ liter salt glaze. 13½" (33.5 cm).

The ample girth of this plumed, 16th century knight is the most distinctive characteristic of this cobalt blue stein. The warrior's costume is profusely decorated with intricate designs. His two stubby arms, scarcely fitting around his bulbous belly, are holding a shield that covers his front. The shield reads, "Iss was gar ist Trink was klar ist Sprich was wahr ist Lieb was rar ist" (Eat what is cooked, drink what is clear, speak what is true, and love what is rare).

A cape pulled over his shoulders and a high, frilled collar are other major features of his outfit. The countenance of the unsmiling knight is embellished with a stylized beard. A twined, rope-like handle is the only portion of the stein that is without the cobalt blue glaze.

The number 58 is the lone mark on the bottom of the vessel. This stein was manufactured by REINHOLD HANKE (18) about 1885.

Fig. 247

KNIGHT. 2 liter stoneware. 13" (32.9 cm).

Similar to the preceding stein. The only differences are very subtle changes in the decorative embellishments. This large vessel has a cream-colored body, with details brought out in blue, black, and green glazes. The shield on the body has the following inscription: "Bier oder Wein, Eins muss es sein" (Beer or wine, one or the other).

Only mold No. 663 appears on the bottom. This vessel was produced by MARZI & REMI (9), about 1890.

Fig. 248

113

KNIGHT. 1½ liter salt glaze. 13¾" (34.7 cm).

Similar to the preceding potbellied knight. Once again there are subtle design changes and a different slogan is inscribed on the shield. This one reads: "Trink nach alter deutscher Weise in der Freunde frohem Kreise lange diesen Krug noch leer" (In the circle of friends, empty this stein in the old German custom). Two grape leaves make up the pewter thumblift.

NO MARKS, only the number 133 is incised on the bottom of this cobalt blue vessel.

Fig. 249

KNIGHT. 2 liter. 14½" (36.7 cm).

A different variation of the preceding vessels. Here the predominant coloring is a highly glazed deep beige in the helmet, uniform, and handle. Deep greens are seen in his beard, cape, and sleeves. The shield reads "Preis and Ruhm dem Gersten saft singt er aus Seel and Liebeskraft" (Praise and glory to the barley brew. He sings with his soul and all his strength!).

NO MARKS, only *Fachschule* (technical school) and *Teplitz* (a city in Bohemia, now Czechoslovakia).

Fig. 250

KNIGHT. 1½ liter pottery. 13" (33 cm).

Here we see a different variation in that the bulbous figure is in blue and white. Delft-like in appearance, with a scene of two sail boats on his frontal portion.

This vessel is marked:

$$\frac{C.S.}{10}$$
13

Fig. 251

114

APPLES

Fig. 252

ADAM AND EVE. 1/8 liter, soft paste porcelain. 2½'' (6.5 cm).

This small stein stands only 2½'' tall and is in the shape of a red and yellow apple. Wrapped around the fruit is a serpent, the tail of which forms the unique handle. The dorsal scales are black with specks of white bordering the brown scutum (underbelly). A forked tongue painted on the apple appears to protrude from the snake's gaping mouth.

NO MARKS.

APPLE. 1/2 liter stoneware.

This exhibits the Art Nouveau style so popular in Europe at the turn of the century. The crimson apple body is capped with a stylized pewter lid and graceful stem thumblift.

The VILLEROY AND BOCH Mercury head trademark appears on the base. Although listed in the Villeroy and Boch 1901 catalogue as having a mold number 2683, this stein was only incised with the date of '04 (16a).

Fig. 253

115

Fig. 254

CUCUMBER. 1/2 liter pottery. 9½" (24 cm).

The lid of this stein has a smiling face of a man who looks like he has a little too much of the hops. In fact, a bit of foam or brew appears to be dribbling out of his mouth. This pickle has arms in the shape of leafy vines. They are brown in color. The right hand or vine is grasping a silver and gray smiling herring.

NO MARKS.

CUCUMBER. 1/2 liter porcelain. 7½" (19 cm).

This unusual dark green stein has a texture much like a real pickle or cucumber. Upon close examination, it is noted that this pickle has a face! The handle is shaped like a fish and is colored in tones of silver and grey. The pewter thumblift connects to the upper end of the pickle.

NO MARKS.

CUCUMBER. 1/2 liter porcelain. 7½" (19 cm).

Vines form the handle as well as the nose on the amusing face. Predominant colors include both light and dark greens, while the stein has accents of pink and white. A large green leaf sits on the pickle's forehead and a smaller leaf serves as the mouth.

This stein has the familiar HASH (1) mark and MUSTERSCHUTZ (10) on the base.

Fig. 255

SAD RADISHES. 3 liter porcelain master *Krug*: 12″ (30.5 cm) to the tips of its leaves; 1/2 liter porcelain: 7½″ (19 cm); 1/3 liter porcelain; 6″ (15.2 cm); 1/20 liter porcelain: 3½″ (8.8 cm).

The body of the *Krug* has spiny root-like hands grasping its stomach. The beige/honey colored stein is incised with brown markings to give the appearance of a natural radish. Two green vines fuse together to form the unique handle. Radishes (*Radieschen*) were to beer drinkers of old Germany what pretzels are today.

A smaller version of this stein is the 1/2 liter one. This tan and beige radish also shows the green delicate leaves on the lid. Its tiny root-like hands wrap under its chin to form the base.

Marked MUSTERSCHÜTZ (10).

Fig. 256

117

Fig. 257

HAPPY RADISH. 1/2 liter porcelain. 7½″ (19 cm).
   Similar to its sad brethren, here its face lights up with a comical broad smile. Size and markings are similar to the Sad Radish.

Fig. 258

Fig. 259

SAD RADISH ON BASE. 1/3 liter. 8½″ (21.5 cm).
   This stein is similar to the prior in coloring and texture. The beige base appears to be the upper part of a beer keg. It was used to support a music box.
   Marked MUSTERSCHUTZ (10).

118

Fig. 260

Fig. 261

HAPPY RADISH. 1/2 liter porcelain. 7½" (19 cm).

A very delicate rendition typical of the Meissen factory. The white base has a pinkish smiling face on its surface. There are two variations of this stein. One version has hand-painted flowers, bees, birds, butterflies, and a dragon on its sides and top. The other is plain, only with the radish markings incised along its sides. A white root with green leaves forms the handle.

Marked with the blue crossed swords of the MEISSEN factory.

Fig. 262

HAPPY RADISH. 1/2 liter. 7½" (19 cm).

Similar to the prior steins, this white stein's face has tears dripping from its eyes. Two small warts are on its stubbled face. Lid has closed leaves on the top; there is no attachment for a handle. The name "Schwinge" written on the lid may indicate the artist.

This stein is also marked with the crossed blue swords of MEISSEN under the handle.

119

HAPPY RADISH. 6½″ (16.5 cm).

A different variation of the other steins, this radish appears to be wearing glasses. A coiled serpent winds around his head to form the lid. The stein is basically a light beige with yellows and greens in the lid and collar.

NO MARKS, only No. 7 57 8 GERMANY incised in the base.

Fig. 263

BISMARK RADISH. 6½″ (16.5 cm).

To complete our radish family, we must have Count Otto Bismark.

For more complete information refer to Famous People. (Fig. 136).

Marked MUSTERSCHUTZ (10).

Fig. 264

ACORN. 1/2 liter pottery. 8'' (20 cm).

This large acorn is decorated in shades of yellow, green, and brown. The handle is shaped like a tree branch or trunk, with two oak leaves on the left of the base and one to the right. Two acorns are hidden by the handle.

NO MARKS, only GERMANY F and mold No. 1235 4.

Fig. 265

EAR OF CORN. 1/2 liter porcelain. 8½'' (21.5 cm).

The kernels of corn are a natural yellow, with bright green husk leaves. The handle and small pouring spout are extensions of the husk leaves.

Unknown manufacturer, but base is marked 801 and

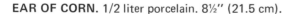

Fig. 266

MEN

Fig. 267

SULKY RACE HORSE DRIVER. 1/2 liter porcelain. 5¾'' (14.7 cm).

The face of this rare stein is totally covered by a face shield with built in green goggles. Only the nostrils and lips are uncovered. The face shield, hood, collar, tie, and coat are colored a dusty gray. The racing cap and visor are dusty orange. A pewter ring holds a ceramic insert which forms the upper portion of the cap.

NO MARKS.

GENTLEMAN SCHOOL TEACHER. 1/2 liter porcelain. 5¾'' (14.6 cm).

This quaint, suave gentleman at first appearance looks like an Englishman. Upon closer examination, and after noting the similarities with the following Heidelberg Student stein, a definite association can be seen.

The texture and workmanship is that of the many steins marked with the HASH (1) and MUSTERSCHUTZ (10) marks. The basic colors are beige/brown, except for the black monocle. The unusual handle is in the shape of a slim face with a long tongue hanging out. This white handle is also seen in the following stein.

Fig. 268

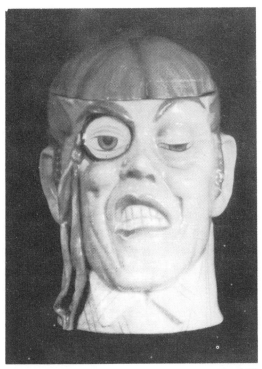

Fig. 269   Fig. 270

HEIDELBERG STUDENT. 1/2 liter porcelain. 5¾'' (14.6 cm).

The prevailing colors are an off-white face, honey-colored hair, and a brown monocle hanging from his right eye. A sneer with his lips reveals his white teeth. Again the handle is white in the shape of a face with a long tongue hanging out.

Marked with the HASH (1) and MUSTERSCHUTZ (10) marks. Also a small number 5.68 along the edge of the base.

TYROLEAN MAN. 1/2 liter bisque. 6½" (16.5 cm).

This finely detailed stein is of a quality and worksmanship seen in the many fine steins crafted by E. BOHNE (2), even though his markings were not seen on this specimen. Colors are skin tones with light brown hair, brown coat, white shirt, red tie, and light green hat. The handle is in the shape of a tied sausage (*wurst*).

NO MARKS only No. 46 on bottom.

Fig. 271

JUDGE. 1/2 liter porcelain. 7" (17.7 cm).

Basic colors of this man of wisdom are the beige/browns associated with the HASH (1) and MUSTERSCHUTZ (10) marks. The pewter-rimmed lid consists of a silver-colored funnel attached to the handle. His braided hair forms a handle with a bow at the end. White collar ruching completes this fine stein.

Fig. 272

FISHERMAN. 3/10 liter bisque. 4¼" (10.8 cm).

This old salt's complexion is ruddy to dark tan, with white eyebrows and beard. His sou'wester cap is gray, and his pipe is brown.

NO MARKS.

Fig. 273

Fig. 274

INDIAN CHIEF. Bisque. 1/2 liter: 7" (17.7 cm); 1/4 liter: 5¼" (14 cm).

A lifelike dedication to the American Indian. The chief's face is a reddish flesh tone. Atop his black hair is the white feathered headdress.

Marked E. BOHNE (2a).

Fig. 275

CHINESE MAN. 3/10 liter porcelain. 4½" (12 cm) to the top of the finial on the hat.

Colors are the usual creams, beiges and light tans associated with steins marked MUSTER-SCHUTZ (10). The braid of his pigtail forms the handle and is looped to complete the base. The pewter thumblift is an array of hops leaves.

Marked MUSTERSCHUTZ (10) GERMANY. Also the numbers 3 10 11 incised in the bottom. A brown 43 was also noted, in glaze on the bottom.

ORIENTAL MAN. 1/2 liter pottery. 7" (17.7 cm).

A pewter hat sits atop his beige head. The inscription around the red base reads, "Sogar im fernen Chinaland das Münchner Bier Yerehrer fand" (Even in the faraway Chinaland, the Munich beer found admirers). Lithophane shows a Munich Maid with a stein in her hand.

Marked J. REINEMANN, MÜNCHEN (13).

Fig. 276

ORIENTAL MAN. 1/2 liter pottery. 5½" (14 cm).

Lid is ringed pewter, symbolizing a coolie's conical hat. The face is painted on the body of the stein. Colors are skin tones, with the mustache and hair in black. His braids form the handle.

The inscription on the rear side reads, "Er trägt den Zopf mit Stolz and Liebe. In Taku bekam er seine hiebe" (He's carrying his braids with pride and love. In Taku, he got worked over.) Taku is a small seaport in northern China near Tientsin.

NO MARKS, only GERMANY.

Fig. 277

Fig. 278

DUELIST. 1 liter pottery. 9″ (23 cm).

Colors are skin tones, brown hair, blue eyes and pink tongue. A high, tan collar forms the bottom which is marked SARREGUEMINES — a city in France — and mold No. 2885.

Fig. 279

STUDENT DUELIST. 1/2 liter porcelain. 7″ (17.7 cm) to the top of the thumblift.

This duelist is attired in his black fraternity garb, with red, black, and white piping. His black eye patch and multiple facial scars indicates indoctrination into the group. His facial colors are skin tones with a brown mustache. The thumblift is the full body of a barmaid holding a tankard of ale. The lithophane depicts a street scene.

Along the edge of the bottom is marked in green under glaze the markings BRÜDER KARAMOZOV MÜNCHEN and GESETZLICH GESCHÜTZT.

Fig. 280

STUDENT. 1/2 liter pottery. 7¼″ (18.4 cm).

Basic colors are flesh tones for his face with brown hair, mustache, and eyebrows. A gray beige cap forms the lid. His neck forms the yellow brown pedestal base.

Marked D.R.G.M. 154927 (3) GERMANY GESETLICH GESCHUTZT 704 B.

126

Fig. 281   Fig. 282

PORTLY BÜRGER. 1/2 liter pottery. 6″ (15.2 cm).

The basic colors of this stein are gray with ruddy facial tones, a brown pipe, and gold pierced earrings. Inscribed along the base is "Die Kehl kost veel" (The throat costs much).

NO MARKS, only GESETZLICH GESCHÜTZ GERMANY.

UNCOMFORTABLE BÜRGER. 1/2 liter pottery. 5¼″ (13.3 cm).

You would grimace too if you had a brown bug crawling down your forehead. Basic colors of this stein are beiges, pinks, browns, and greens. A pewter lid forms the small hat on his head.

NO MARKS only mold No. 142 G and small No. 28 GERMANY.

Fig. 283

BEARDED KNIGHT'S HEAD. 1/2 liter pottery. 7½″ (19 cm).

This salt glaze, oval-shaped vessel has colors that are primarily blue and light beige. His pointed head, with a lock of brown hair on top, forms the lid of this comical stein. A small medal dangles from his neck.

In a rectangular box, on the bottom, is the marking MUSTERSCHUTZ D & B, Nº 46. DÜMLER & BREIDEN. (19).

127

SULTAN. 4/10 liter porcelain 5" (12.7 cm).

    The era of Kismet is portrayed in this beautiful stein. Colors are flesh tones with a dark brown beard. His turban is checked in red and blue small patterns. A blue gem is in front. A pewter lid sits on his head, attached to the large acorn thumblift.

    NO MARKS.

Fig. 284

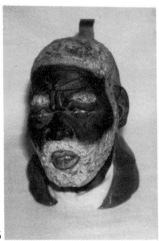

BLACK MAN. 1/2 liter bisque porcelain. 6" (15.2 cm).

    Basic color of this stein is black, with gray hair and beard. His red jacket and white collar are in a glazed porcelain finish.

    NO MARKS, only No. 26.29 written on the bottom.

Fig. 285

GRIMACING MAN. 1/2 liter pottery. 6½" (16.5 cm).

    Here we see a large beetle atop his head. Evidently he's had a few too many for the road. His skin-toned ruddy face has brown eyebrows with dark pink flowing around his hair.

    NO MARKS, only mold No. 693 GERMANY GES. GESCH.

Fig. 286

IMP. 1 liter bronze pouring stein. 9½" (24 cm).

    This Art Nouveau stein consists of a **smiling** faced imp. The handle is of a nude woman. Weighing 9 pounds, this French beauty is signed E. LaPORTE DORE.

Fig. 287

HOPS LADY. 1/2 liter porcelain. 6″ (15.2 cm).

Her beautiful face with downcast eyes is wreathed by hair fashioned from hops buds. On top of the hairdo is a crown of leaves from the hops plant. The handle is formed from the trunk of the hops vines. Coloring of this stein is various shades of honey and beige. The hops leaves are a pale green.

Marked with the HASH (1) and MUSTER-SCHUTZ (10) marks.

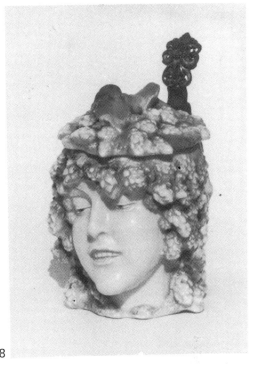

Fig. 288

HOPS LADY. 1/2 liter pottery. 6″ (15.2 cm).

Basic colors are brown hair, green hops leaves, yellow hops, and flesh-toned face with rosy cheeks. Below her chin is the inscription, "Prosit!"

Marked mold No. 1424 GERMANY GESETZLICH GESCHUTZT.

Fig. 289

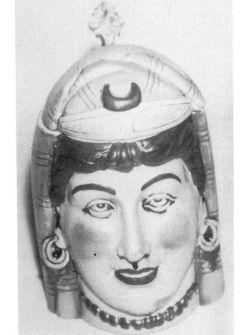

EGYPTIAN LADY. 1/2 liter pottery. 6″ (15.2 cm).

This colorful stein is highlighted by deep brown hair and red beads and crescent. Her headdress is shaded in varying tones of green and yellow.

Marked ECKHARDT & ENGLER KG (6a). GERMANY Mold No. 431.

Fig. 290

COQUETTE. 1/2 liter pottery. 8'' (20.3 cm).

Basic colors of this young woman's face are beige and black. A blue ribbon wraps through her hair. Her braided hair is upswept to form part of the lid. A small flower dangles from her smiling mouth. There must be spring in the air.

NO MARKS, only mold No. 766.

Fig. 291

CAROLINE. 1/2 liter porcelain. 6'' (15.2 cm).

Basic colors of this delicate woman are the beige/browns and whites associated with the MUSTERSCHUTZ (10) mark. This young lady is wearing two strands of gold beads around her neck, above her white ruffled collar. A gold and white rope with tassles wraps around her hat.

Fig. 292

Fig. 293

SMILING WOMAN. 1/2 liter porcelain. 7'' (17.7 cm).

This lovely young lady's face is toned in a ''peaches and cream complexion'', with blue eyes. Her reddish-brown hair gathers in the back to form the handle. The face is set off by a blue bow around her neck and a matching ribbon in her hair.

Marked MUSTERSCHUTZ (10) and the HASH (1) marks.

130

Fig. 294

MASQUERADE LADY. 1/2 liter porcelain. 8½" (21.5 cm).

This beautiful young woman's face is adorned by a black lace mask and a white ruffled collar to show a hint of her costume. Her light brown curled hair is swept back to form the handle of this most delicate, lovely stein. Masquerade parties were quite common among the royalty during the late 19th century.

Marked MUSTERSCHUTZ (10) and a small number 3.58.

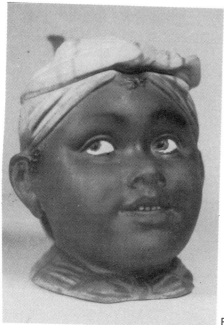

BLACK GIRL. 1/4 liter bisque porcelain. 4¾" (12 cm).

This delicate bisque bust has rosy chocolate skin tones set off by large white eyes. Kerchief and neckerchief are an off-white with contrasting red and blue stripings.

NO MARKS.

Fig. 295

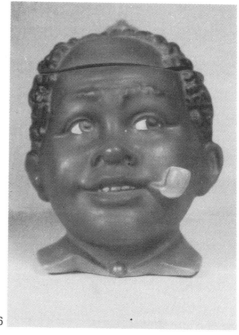

BLACK BOY. 1/4 liter bisque porcelain. 4¾" (12 cm).

Mate to the Black Girl. Similar chocolate skin tones and a **yellow** pipe set off this handsome lad. Black **nair** and a beige collar completes this fine stein.

NO MARKS.

Fig. 296

132

Fig. 297

ALPINE HUNTER; 1/2 liter porcelain. 6¾" (17 cm) to the top of the chamois thumblift.

Coloring of this Tyrolean man varies from the deep green of his hat and collar to the flesh tones of his face, which is accented by the black mustache, eyebrows, and hair. A lithophane depicts a man and woman dancing.

NO MARKS, only GES on the back of his collar.

ALPINE WOMAN. 1/2 liter porcelain. 6½" (16.5 cm).

Mate to the preceding stein. Basic colors are the flesh tones of her face, black hair, deep green hat with a yellow stripe, and green collar with pink bow at neck. Her hair is braided to form the handle. A strap marked NBM attaches the pewter-ringed lid to the handle. The thumb-lift consists of a man with a stein in one hand and his doffed hat in the other. The lithophane of this stein is similar to its mate.

NO MARKS, only gaf. gefyl. written along the edge of the bottom.

Fig. 298

Fig. 299

OLD MAN. 1/2 liter semi-glazed porcelain. 6" (15.2 cm).

Color is a varying cream and white. The pewterless lid forms his bald head. The handle is in the shape of a tree trunk.

Marked MUSTERSCHUTZ (10).

Fig. 300

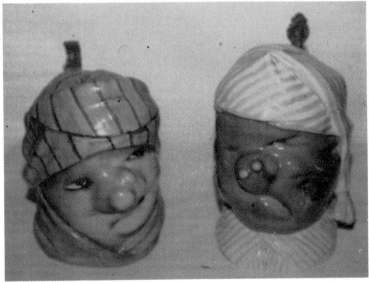

Fig. 301

POTATO FACE. 1/2 liter porcelain. 5 1/2" (14 cm).

The lowly potato is the basis for the face of this peasant. Indentations are used to depict the eyes and mouth, while protrusions are utilized for the nose, chin, and wart on his nose. The face is the color of a light tan Idaho potato. The turban is blue and yellow stripes, which continues to form the handle. His neckerchief is a light green with a floral design.

Marked with the HASH (1) and MUSTER-SCHUTZ (10) markings.

POTATO FACE WITH NIGHTCAP. 1/2 liter porcelain. 6½" (16.5 cm).

This mate to the preceding is wearing a blue and white striped shirt and nightcap. His handle is green to indicate the vine of the potato plant.

Marked MUSTERSCHUTZ (10).

Fig. 302

Fig. 303

FOOTBALL MAN. 1/2 liter pottery. 6'' (15.4 cm).

This football-shaped stein has a beige cap, ruddy-cheeked face, brown hair and eyebrows, red lips, and brown highlighting.

On the bottom MADE IN GERMANY is printed with an incised mold No. 426.

MAN IN THE MOON. 4/10 liter porcelain. 7'' (17.7 cm).

This happy fellow is in the shape of a half moon, the handle consists of an old fashioned key. Coloring is varying shades of cream and tan.

Marked E. BOHNE (2a).

PAN. 1/2 liter porcelain. 5½'' (14 cm).

This delicate glazed stein has flesh tones with brown hair, red lips, rust and maroon grapes, and leaves around his forehead. The porcelain lid which forms his cap is laden with bunches of purple grapes and green leaves and vines. Marked CAPO-di-MONTE (17).

Fig. 304

Fig. 305

Fig. 306

PIXIE. 1/2 liter porcelain. 7½" (19 cm).

This stein is a head of an imp or elf. The head is capped with a soft peaked hat. A garland of meadow daisies rings the pixie's head. Huge eyes and ears are the most distinguishing characteristics of the face. The pupils of the intriguing eyes are elliptical, characteristic of nocturnal animals. A "Peter Pan" type collar and a fancy handle finish off the decorative aspects of the stein. The pewter thumblift is plain.

The colors of this stein are the usual beige/honey colors commonly associated with the HASH (1) and MUSTERSCHUTZ (10) marks.

PIXIE. 1/2 liter porcelain. 9½" (24 cm).

Very similar to the prior, here we see the same elf sitting on top of a deep base, possibly for a music box. The high base contributes to its height. Same beige/honey coloring.

Marked MUSTERSCHUTZ (10).

Fig. 307

JUDGE. 1/2 liter porcelain. 7¼" (18.4 cm).

Here we find our little pixie pouring knowledge into the head of a perplexed judge. With finger to the side of his nose, our magistrate is certainly weighing a difficult decision. His light beige robe is encircled with a white ruffled collar. His darker beige wig matches the coloring of the pixie's peaked hat and waist coat. The silver funnel is the color of the elf's pants. The unique handle is an extension from the judge in the shape of a light beige pigtail.

This humorous stein is marked MUSTERSCHUTZ (10).

Fig. 308

JESTER. 1/2 liter porcelain. 10" (25.4 cm).

A most unusual pitcher, the white base is ornately decorated with colorful red, beige, and yellow foliage. A smiling, impish, jester's face peers out of the pewter lid. His skin-toned face is accented by blushing reddish nose and cheeks. His droopy jester's cap is striped blue and white, with a jagged red line.

Marked:

137

CLOWN WITH BANJO. 1 liter pottery. 9¼" (23.5 cm).

A very colorful, brightly painted stein. His hat, which forms the lid, is lavender and gold. His skin-toned face is set off with a bushy brown mustache. The clown attire consists of a lavender shirt with a green collar and billowy pants of bright red. On either side of the base are seen three dogs (a dachshund on the left; a beagle and a gray poodle on the right).

Two small plaques are on either side of the handle. They are inscribed, "Bei Trunk u. Scherz bleibt froh das Herz" (With drink and humor the heart stays happy) and "Im Leid und Leben nach Einheit streben" (In song and life look for unity).

The small number 721 is inscribed just below the handle. The same mold number is on the base. Also GESETZLICH GESCHÜTZT GERMANY. This stein is a mate to the Clown with Concertina.

Fig. 309

CLOWN WITH CONCERTINA. 1 liter pottery. 9¾" (24.8 cm).

This stein is the mate to the preceding. His three-tiered clown's hat is pink, green, and brown. His costume is pink with grey ruffing. Large pink flowers, with green leaves are seen along the rear of the stein.

This stein has the same markings as above, mold No. 748.

Fig. 311

Fig. 310

MAN WITH JESTER'S HAT. 2 liter pottery. 14½" (36.8 cm).

This large, humorous stein has an over-proportioned head, topped by a pewter rimmed, yellow jester's hat. His brown eyes are peering skyward, perhaps towards the drinker? His bright red vest has a light blue collar peeking out. A brown coat, beige slacks, and green grass complete the front of this colorful *krug.* The back shows flowers and leaves to compliment the handle which consists of one snake eating another.

Marked D.R.G.M. 154327 (3) mold No. 719, GES. GESCH GERMANY.

MAN WITH JESTER'S HAT. 1½ liter pottery. 13½" (34 cm).

Similar in texture and coloring to the prior stein, the body of the stein is encased in a gold-stippled brown background. Here our happy man is wearing a brownish-yellow outfit with green shirt and red bow tie. His conical shaped hat is red, yellow, purple, and green. On the back surface are purple flowers and green leaves.

The number 752 is incised to the left of the handle. The base is marked D.R.G.M. (3) 154927 GESETZLICH GESCHÜTZT GERMANY. Mold No. H151.

Fig. 312

JESTER. 1/4 liter pottery. 6¼" (15.8 cm).

This small stein is very similar in appearance to the previous specimen. His four-sided hat is colored pink, blue, yellow, and red, with a brown band. The costume is a reddish brown with gray ruffing around the neck and sleeves. His whimsical face is skin-toned with a brown mustache and rosy cheeks.

On the rear of the base are two flower-lined panels inscribed: "Froh beim Bier" (Happy with beer) and "Das lieben wir" (That we love).

The number 792 is incised under the handle, which corresponds to mold No. 792 found on the bottom. Marked D.R.G.M. 15 . . . (indiscernible) . . . GES. GESCHUTZT.

Fig. 313

Fig. 314

CLOWN. 1 liter pottery. 9½" (24 cm).

Texture and color of this stein are similar to the preceding Jester. The costume is a brownish yellow, with a gray ruffled collar and cuffs. It is larger in size, but has the same inscription on the rear panels. "Froh beim Bier das lieben wir."

NO MARKS, only GES. GESCH. GER. Mold No. 750.

CLOWN. 1/2 liter porcelain. 6½" (16.5 cm).

This sad faced clown has a whitened face, which is accented by his red nose and lips. The unusual handle is formed by an inverted jester. The lid is attached to the jester's legs by a pewter thumblift in the shape of a smiling half moon. The detailed lithophane depicts two bowing clowns, tipping their hats to each other. They are holding canes or walking sticks.

NO MARKS.

Fig. 315

Fig. 316

CLOWN. 1/2 liter pottery. 10" (25.4 cm).

Strutting along in his baggy, striped, beige and brown costume, this happy clown has a square beige plaque on his stomach inscribed, "Trink aus meinem-bauch, dein Bier in deinen Schlauch" (Drink your beer out of my belly into your throat).

Even though there are NO MARKS, this stein has been identified in the REINHOLD HANKE (18) catalog. Mold No. 987 incised.

Fig. 317

CLOWN. 1/2 liter pottery. 6¾'' (17 cm).

The yellow, gray, black, pink, and beige stripes are colorfully painted on the stoneware surface.

NO MARKS only mold No. 1570.

Fig. 318

CLOWN. 1/2 liter pottery. 7½'' (19 cm).

The lid consists of a large ruffled clown's collar and his whitened smiling face.

The glazed pottery body is marked on the base MERKELBACH AND WICK (4a).

Fig. 319

JESTER. 4/10 liter porcelain. 6¼'' (15.8 cm).

Here our frustrated jester is gazing with crossed eyes at the horsefly sitting on his nose. His anguish is evidenced by his tight lips and bit tongue. Coloring of this stein varies from the white of his high shirt collar to the light beige of his skin. His pointed hat rests on the pewter ring of the lid.

The attaching strap is marked NBM. Marked E. BOHNE (2a). Mold No. 8469.

141

CLOWN. 1/4 liter pottery. 6¾'' (17 cm).

Another very colorful depiction of a cheery clown, from the beige bottom to the top of his pink hat. Two rear panels read, ''Die alten Deutschen tranken'' (The old Germans drank) and ''Noch Eins ehe sie gingen'' (One more before they went).

NO MARKS, only the incised mold number 766 and GESETZLICH GESCHÜTZT GERMANY.

Fig. 320

WOMAN WITH JESTER'S HAT. 1/2 liter pottery. 8½'' (21.2 cm).

Colors are bright with flesh-tone face, brown hair, and yellow pedestal base. The pewter-ringed lid forms the blue, pink, and yellow jester's hat.

NO MARKS, only mold No. 702 GES. GESCH.

Fig. 321

MILITARY HEAD. 1/2 liter porcelain. 7½'' (19 cm).

The head depicts a Bavarian soldier. The model 1868 **Raupenhelm** (wool-top helmet) is characteristic of Bavaria and the gothic *L* is for ''Mad'' King Ludwig II (1864-1886). After Ludwig's death, the *raupenhelm* was changed to conform to the Prussian pattern and a new helmet device, the coat of arms flanked by lion retainers, was used instead of the *L*. The pompon is normally mounted on the helmet's left side. This helmet with the *L* replaced an earlier model with an *M* for King Maximilian, Ludwig's father.

The stein is colored in the usual brown/beiges associated with the green MUSTERSCHUTZ (10) printed on the base.

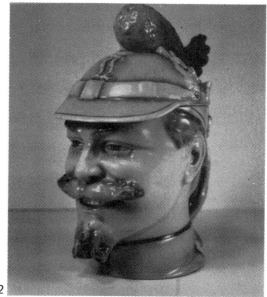

Fig. 322

PRUSSIAN INFANTRY CADET-OFFICER. 1/2 liter porcelain. 7½'' (19 cm) to the top of the spike.

The helmet is similar to the 1867-style *Garde* helmet found on the Bismark steins (see Famous People). However, the front visor is rounded, rather than angled.

Again we see the varying shades of beige/brown with the inscription MUSTERSCHUTZ (10) and the numbers 34 and 6.

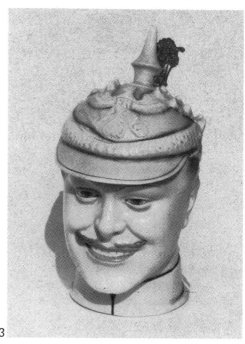

Fig. 323

143

Fig. 324

Fig. 325

ENLISTED MAN. 1/2 liter glazed porcelain. 6½" (16.5 cm) to the top of the red and white *mutze* (cap).

The character is a *kurassier* in undress uniform, used for "walking out" dress. The *koller* has double rows of gold tresses on the front. The hat color indicates the man is from either of the following regiments -- Garde du Corps, 2nd, or 4th kurassiere. All wore the same type hat, but colors differed between the regiments. The double pips (*Landes*) and *Reich-skokarde,* indicate a uniform of post-1897 to 1910. The face is in flesh-tones with a black mustache, eyebrows, and hair.

NO MARKS.

ENLISTED MAN. 1/2 liter porcelain. 6" (15 cm).

Similar in texture to above, this stein depicts a member of the Saxon Garde Reiter, an elite cavalry unit of Saxony, who took a lion-topped helmet for parade. He too wears a *koller* of blue and white.

NO MARKS, but the No. S 1195 appears on the pewter thumblift.

BRITISH SAILOR. 0.15 liter porcelain. 3-3/8" (8.6 cm).

Colors are flesh-tones for face, with blue eyes and dark blue collar. Hat is white with black band.

NO MARKS.

Fig. 326

GERMAN OFFICER. 1/2 liter pottery. 7¾" (19.7 cm).

A German officer wearing "off duty" or *Offiziers mutze* cap. The uniform is styled along the lines of the typical Army land uniform and is otherwise devoid of any insignia indicative of high rank. There is a resemblance to Bismark, but this identification is considered unlikely. The stein has an overall purple/gray color.

NO MARKS.

Fig. 327

SOLDIER. 1/2 liter salt glaze. 7" (17.7 cm).

A blue and gray bust of soldier. The cap appears to be a Swiss pattern. The uniform could be of any European power since all use the stand-up collar.

The initials LB&C are incised in the base along with "geset. gesch." (15).

Fig. 328

Fig. 329

Fig. 330

Fig. 331

SAILOR. 1 liter pottery. 12" (30.5 cm).

This most unusual figurine depicts a slightly tipsy sailor sitting atop an ornate keg. The keg has a very colorful picture of his ship on the front (the S.M.S. *Nassau,* which is also written across his hatband). A picture of the ship S.M.S. *Hessen* is seen on the back panel. Along either side of the barrel are two sailors holding rifles between their legs (undoubtedly guarding the liquid refreshments). The sailor is holding an empty mug (dated 1908-11) in his right hand, a black walking stick in his left.

Inscribed along the base is "Brüder stosst die Gläser an" (Brother, clink your glasses). On the rear base is "Es lebe der Reservemann" (Long live the reservist). The plain cream-colored handle is topped by a pewter bird for a thumblift. The inscription "Reserve hat Ruh" (Reservist has rest) is written on the handle. On the periphery of the front panel is also written, "Zur Erinnerung am. Dienstzeit b.d. Kaiserl. Marine" (In memory of the service in the Royal Marine). The reservist's name (Res. Dörbaiun) appears on the front of the stein.

The markings D.R.G.M. (3) No. 1007, Coblenz, Gesgesch (15).

146

Fig. 332

SAILOR. 1/2 liter pottery. 8½" (21.5 cm).

This casual "gob" has a brown cigar in his hand. His blue uniform is offset by the white blouse and black shoes.

NO MARKS, only GERMANY 1821 13.

ARTILLERY SHELL. 1/2 liter porcelain. 9½″ (24 cm).

This dark blue artillery shell has a beige timing band. The timing band is calibrated with brown numbers to indicate the amount of time until detonation (4-6-8 . . . 44). The pewter cannonball thumblift is inscribed with the letters N.B.M. Lithophane depicts three men sitting around a table playing cards. NO MARKS.

Fig. 333

ARTILLERY SHELL. 1/2 liter porcelain. 9½″ (24 cm).

Similar to above, this artillery shell is colored gray and rust. The gold timing band has a small dial for arming the device. The handle once again is incised with N.B.M. This lithophane shows two women and one man. One of the women is sitting, the other standing.
NO MARKS.

Fig. 334

Fig. 335

ARTILLERY SHELL. 1/2 liter pottery. 10″ (25.4 cm).

This gray stein is inscribed with the major artillery battles of 1914: "Luttich Namur Antwerpen Longwy Maubeuge etc." The inscription on the lid reads 42 cm Geschoss, which translates to 42 cm projectile, indicating the size of the shell. Two brown pressure bands encircle the lower third of the stein.

The letters P.A. and the number 441546 are found on the base.

ARTILLERY SHELL. 1 liter pottery. 16" (42 cm).

The same stein is found in the 1 liter size with the dates 1914/15 on the lid. This stein measures 42 cm, the same as the actual missile. Coloring is beige with two black pressure bands at base.

NO MARKS.

Fig. 336

ARTILLERY SHELL. 1/2 liter pewter. 8¼" (21 cm).

This unusual stein is incised with the First Class Iron Cross. Three horizontal pressure bands appear to be "blued" to the metal (as in the processing of the actual missile).

NO MARKS.

Fig. 337

MISSILE. 1/2 liter pewter. 8½" (21.5 cm).

This stein is inscribed with the Bavarian Crest on its front. The pewter thumblift shows the Iron Cross seen on the front of the prior missile.

This stein has the initials RTM incised in the bottom. Also GES. GESCH. Schutz Marke. (15).

Fig. 338

MONKS

SMILING MONK. 1 liter salt glaze pottery. 9"
(22.9 cm).

The robe and skull cap are blue and gray,
while his face is beige in color. This happy
fellow is clasping a rosary in his right hand,
while his left holds a bible or prayer book.

Marked MERKELBACH & WICK (4a) on
base.

Fig. 339

MONK. 1/2 liter salt glaze pottery. 7" (17.7
cm).

This pious monk has a salt glaze finish in
blues and grays. The pewter thumblift has a
face on it, while a cross hangs from the rope
belt tied around the monk's middle.

Marked MERKELBACH & WICK (4a).

Fig. 340

MONK. 1/2 liter salt glaze pottery. 7½" (19.1
cm).

This monk is almost identical to the preceding stein. It is primarily of a blue purple color.
He appears to be smiling. While the body of this
stein is similar to the preceding stein, the top or
lid which forms the monk's head is different.

Marked MERKELBACH & WICK (4a) on
base.

Fig. 341

MONK. 1/2 liter salt glaze pottery. 7" (17.7 cm).

Once again, a manufacturer produced a monk stein which utilizes a common base or body. As can be seen, this monk's head is substantially different than the previously pictured examples. This pensive fellow sports a full brown beard and is wearing a blue grey hood which matches his robe.

Marked MERKELBACH & WICK (4a) on base.

Fig. 342

MONK. 1/2 liter salt glaze pottery. 6¼" (15.8 cm).

Virtually the same as the preceding stein, this monk is colored the typical gray purple. It is distinguished from the other MERKELBACH & WICK monk steins in that is has a protective pewter ring around its base.

Marked MERKELBACH & WICK (4a) on base.

Fig. 343

Fig. 344

GRINNING MONK. 1/2 liter salt glaze pottery. 7¼" (19.1 cm).

This monk has a purple and gray robe and cap. His face is gray with blue eyes, while the simple handle and his hands are gray.

The manufacturer of this stein is unknown. However there is a small flower in the shape of an edelweis and the number 112 incised on the base.

MONK. 1/2 liter salt glaze pottery. 7¾" (19.7 cm).

This monk was manufactured by the same factory as the previous stein. Two ham hocks hang from the monk's right arm, while two fowl hang from his left. The monk's bearded face is gray with blue eyes, while his robe and cap are purple gray in color.

The unusual edelweis flower and the number 59 are incised on the base.

Fig. 345

MONK. 1/2 liter salt glaze pottery. 7½" (19.1 cm).

This monk is wearing a skull cap and what looks like a bath or smoking robe. The stein is colored in the typical blue and gray salt glaze manner.

There are NO MARKS on the base.

MONK. 1/2 liter salt glaze pottery. 7½" (19.1 cm).

This figure stein is possibly a monk. The stein is predominantly blue gray in color. The monk's beard and cap are brown.

NO MARKS.

Fig. 346

Fig. 347

152

SMILING MONK. 1/2 liter salt glaze pottery. 6¼" (15.8 cm).

This fellow is grasping his rotund stomach, as in the manner of most monk steins. The stein is gray with a purple gray robe.

NO MARKS, only mold No. 194.

Fig. 348

Fig. 349

SMILING MONK. 1/2 liter salt glaze pottery. 6½" (16.5 cm).

The face of this stein is very similar to the last one. This monk's skullcap is striped. The stein is colored in typical blue gray salt glaze manner. The thumblift of this particular example is a running dwarf holding a box under his left arm.

Manufacturer is unknown, but base is marked "OCT".

MONK. 1/2 liter salt glaze pottery. 7½" (19.1 cm).

The face, hands, and base are gray in color, while the rope is brown. A blue strip encircles the base. This hooded monk is dated "1880" on the pewter ring surrounding his head and shoulders, giving some indication as to its age.

NO MARKS.

Fig. 350

GRINNING MONK. 1/2 liter pottery. 7'' (17.7 cm).

This jovial fellow is wearing a black habit and skull cap with a striped cord tie at the waist. His face is beige in color, with red lips and cheeks. The base is encircled with brown and gold stripes.

Manufacturer is unknown, but base has "GERMANY 67" embossed on the bottom.

Fig. 351

Fig. 352

MONK. 1/2 liter.

He carries a large overflowing beer stein in his left hand, while his right clutches a prayer book or Bible. His flowing robe is various shades of brown, the beer stein is gray with white foam, and the Bible has black covers with gold leaf page edges. Our monk is obviously enjoying his brew, as his cheeks are a healthy pink and his smile is one of contentment.

Manufacturer is unknown, but base has on it.

154

MONK. 1/2 liter painted pottery. 5½'' (14 cm).

This squat or egg-shaped monk is holding a stein in his left hand. The monk is pointing with his right forefinger to the foaming stein. A prayer book is also tucked under this bespectacled, smiling fellow's left arm. The stein is mostly black with brown tones. The monk's face forms the domed lid in a pewter rim.

NO MARKS, only mold No. 1574 GERMANY.

Fig. 353

MONK. 1/2 liter porcelain. 7'' (17.7 cm).

He wears a rust colored robe with a white cord tied around his waist, while his skull cap is black. This monk's face is skin-toned with red lips and pink cheeks. The thumblift is in the form of a lyre. There is a lithophane of a man and a woman dancing in a tavern.

NO MARKS.

Fig. 354

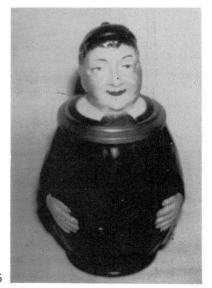

MONK. 1/2 liter porcelain. 7'' (17.7 cm).

This young monk is wearing a reddish brown robe and cap. His hands and face are skin-tone, while his hair is black.

NO MARKS.

Fig. 355

155

Fig. 356

MONK. 1/2 liter stoneware. 6½" (16.5 cm).

This stein is unusual in that the top, which forms the monk's head, is made of bronze. Evidently the original pottery lid was replaced.
NO MARKS.

Fig. 357

MONK. 1/2 liter stoneware. 6½" (16.5 cm).

Identical to the preceding stein. However, it has a blue salt glaze finish.
NO MARKS.

MONK. 1/2 liter pewter. 6½" (16.5 cm).

Similar in design to his pottery brethren, this smiling monk is made entirely of pewter. It has a very heavy and unusual thumblift and hinge.
NO MARKS.

Fig. 358

TIPSY MONK. 1/2 liter bisque porcelain; 6¾″ (17 cm). 1/4 liter also.

   The prevailing colors are an ivory face and a reddish-brown cowl. His tongue is hanging from his mouth in a tipsy manner.

   Marked ERNST BOHNE (2a).

Fig. 359

MONK. 1/2 liter pottery. 7¼″ (18.4 cm).

   His portly, happy face indicates a satisfaction with the world. Tucked into his right hand is a beige stein. In his left is a large black radish. The banner across his chest reads "Wer Bier trinkt schläft gut, Wer gut schläft sündiget nicht. Wer nicht sündigt kommt in den Himmel" (He who drinks beer sleeps well. He who sleeps well cannot sin. He who does not sin gets to heaven). The predominant colors are a glazed cream for his skin-tones to a brown for his robes. A cream vine loops down from his back to form the handle.

   NO MARKS, only mold No. 572. Identified in DÜMLER & BREIDEN (19).

Fig. 360

NUN. 1/2 liter pottery. 6¾″ (17 cm).

The stein is predominantly tan in color with black accents. The nun's cuffs, belt, and rosary under her left arm are all painted black. Her habit and hood are done in a distinctive wavy brown pattern.

The base of this stein is marked "716" and "30". NO MARKS.

Fig. 361

Fig. 362

NUN and **MONK.** 0.4 liter pottery. 6″ (15.2 cm).

Both the Monk and the Nun share identical bodies: only the tops, or heads, are different. Both pottery steins are brown and tan in color. A dark brown or black ring circles the base of both steins.

Marked MERKELBACH & WICK (4a).

NUN. 1/4 liter pottery. 7'' (17.7 cm).

She is wearing a black habit and hood which is slightly highlighted with tan coloring. Her wimple (collar) and cord tie are white, while her smiling face is skin-toned with red cheeks and lips. The base is red and white and the plain handle beige.

Stein was manufactured by REINHOLD HANKE (18) and has "GERMANY" and mold No. "462" incised on bottom of its base.

Fig. 363

NUN. 1/2 liter porcelain. 7'' (17.7 cm).

The habit and hood are black while her wimple and waist cord tie are white. This smiling nun's face is flesh colored with red cheeks and lips while her eyes are blue. The interesting thumblift consists of a dwarf kneeling on a barrel, holding a stein with beer pouring from it. This stein has a large lithophane which depicts a man with arm on shoulder of woman with downcast eyes, who is wearing necklace with cross.

NO MARKS.

Fig. 364

159

NUN. 1/2 liter porcelain. 7" (17.7 cm).

Her habit and hood are black, while her wimple and cord tie are white. Hands and face are skin-toned with red lips. Lithophane in the base depicts a Tyrolean man and woman dancing in tavern. This nun is very similar to the preceding example; however, the base is flared.

NO MARKS.

Fig. 365

NUN. 1/2 liter porcelain. 7½" (19.1 cm).

The stein is unusual in that the nun's head is made of bronze or copper. Her habit is rust red while her hands and sash are white. This stein has a lithophane of a man and woman embracing.

NO MARKS.

Fig. 366

Fig. 367

The Münchner Kindl (Munich Child) is the symbol of both Munich and Bavaria. It began as the Munich coat of arms in 1239 and has since evolved from a hooded monk standing in front of Munich's gates to a charming child (almost always shown as female) dressed in hood and cape and holding a stein of beer and, usually, a bunch of radishes.

MUNICH CHILD. 1/2 liter bisque porcelain. 8½" (21.5 cm).

This Child is basically black with blue linings inside the surplice and around the cuffs. The surplice itself is beige. The figure has a lovely face with light brown hair. There is a white panel at the rear of the stein with MARTIN PAUSON, MÜNCHEN written on it. Twin domes thumblift. Lithophane depicts a city scene with people, a church, and city buildings (possibly Munich).

Fig. 368

MUNICH CHILD. 1/4 liter porcelain. 6¾" (17 cm).

The robe, pointed cowl, and base of stein are black. The scapular is yellow. Linings of cowl and cuffs are gray blue. The shoes, which peek from under the robe, are red. The face is painted in flesh tones, the hair is blonde. In its left hand the *Münchner Kindl* holds a single green-topped radish. There is no protective pewter rim around shoulders and head. Twin tower thumblift. Lithophane depicts a marketplace scene.

Decorated by MARTIN PAUSON of Munich (14).

Fig. 369

MUNICH CHILD. 1/2 liter pottery. 10" (25.4 cm).

This *Kindl* wears a black robe and hood. Linings of the hood and cuffs are red. The dark yellow surplice (scapular) is in the shape of a cross. The Child is holding a shield on which the twin domes of the Frauenkirche Church of Munich are outlined in pale tan on a red background. The saying "Grus aus München" (Greetings from Munich) is written on it. A beige banner at the base reads "Wohlbekomms" (To your health).

NO MARKS, only the letter *F* incised on bottom.

Fig. 370

162

MUNICH CHILD. 1/2 liter porcelain. 8'' (20.3 cm).

In the shape of a cream-colored barrel, this stein has the Child's head rising out of the barrel. She wears a pointed brown cowl with pale blue lining. The cuff linings are the same. Light brown hair, skin-toned face, with rosy cheeks complete the lid. Sleeves and robe are a dark brown, with tiny red slippers peeking out the bottom. The Child holds a gray stein by its body in her right hand, while her left holds a wooden stein. This wooden stein is often missing. Some beige radishes are tucked under arm. Twin domes thumb-lift. The large lithophane depicts the famous Bavarian Lion inside the garden of the Munich Hofbräuhaus.

Marked with the HASH (1) mark, also MUSTER-SCHUTZ (10) and MARTIN PAUSON, MÜNCHEN (14).

Fig. 371

Bavarian Lion, found inside the garden of the Hofbräuhaus in Munich.

MUNICH CHILD. 1/2 liter porcelain. 7½'' (19 cm).

Overall coloring of body and cowl is black. Cowl lining, one cuff, and scapular are yellow-to-gold colored. At bottom of the scapular is a blue panel in which the figure's name "Müncher Kindl" (Munich Child) is written in old English script. The Child holds a Bible with a cross on it in its right hand. The face is flesh-toned with blue eyes, red mouth and brownish hair. Head and shoulders, which form the lid of the stein, are edged with a pewter rim.

The lithophane depicts the Statue of Bavaria with the Bavarian lion in front of the Ruhmeshalle (Hall of Glory). Both are famous Munich Landmarks. (See "Bavaria" in Figurals.)

The decorating and pewter shop of MARTIN PAUSON (14) did the painting and pewter work. His name and München appear in a white panel at the base, near the handle.

Fig. 372

MUNICH CHILD. 1/2 liter porcelain. 7'' (17.7 cm).

This appears to be very similar to previous stein in overall coloring. Different features are the pointed hood, missing blue panel at the bottom of the scapular, and lack of the decorator's name. Lithophane of Statue of Bavaria.

Fig. 373

Fig. 374

Fig. 375

MUNICH CHILD. Earthenware. 1/8 liter, 5-3/8" (13.5 cm). 1/4 liter, 6-3/8" (16.1 cm). 1/2 liter, 8" (20 cm). 1 liter, 10" (25 cm).

Best known and most common of all *Münchner Kindl* or Munich Maid steins, this cream colored character comes in numerous sizes.

Body and cowl are black, scapular yellow to tan, radishes have green tops. The *Kindl* holds a large lidded HB (for Hofbraühaus brewery) stein. The name of the city, München or Munich, appears in green letters on a cream colored stein. A pewter rim with coin notching on its outer edge encases the head which has the cowl drawn up over it, forming the stein's top. The face is painted in flesh tones, with rosy cheeks and blue eyes. White teeth can be seen through the red lips and the hair is brown. Some steins have faces devoid of coloring except for black eyes. Expressions on the faces vary according to different artist-painters. Cowl linings can be either gold leaf or green, or both.

Favorite thumblifts for this stein are in the shape of the Frauenkirche twin domes (Church of Our Lady), a well-known Munich landmark; other lifts are not unusual.

Impressed in bottom is the name, J. REINE-MANN, a decorating shop in Munich. GESETZ-LICH GESCHÜTZT also appears on the bottom.

165

MUNICH CHILD. 1/2 liter porcelain, 8'' (20.3 cm). 1½ ounce, 4'' (10 cm).

The robe is black with gold linings and gold scapular. Slippers and buttons are a bright red. The Child is seen holding two radishes in her right hand and a large pretzel tucked under her arm. Radishes are tucked into the scapular over her left arm. The lid seems out of proportion to the base, as though the Child were wearing shoulder pads. Her saintly face is lifted skyward.

In the 1/2 liter size, the lithophane is of the Statue of Bavaria. In the 1½ ounce size, the lithophane shows a Bavarian square.

Marked JOSEPH M. MAYER (12) and GESETZLICH GESCHUTZ.

Fig. 376

MUNICH CHILD. 1/2 liter porcelain. 8½'' (21.5 cm).

Her robe is black, with scapular and cowl linings in gold leaf. Sleeves are white, as is the belt. The Child holds two radishes with green tops. Two red slippers peek out from her robes. Her beautiful, serene face is flesh-toned with teeth showing, cute dimples, and brown hair. A pewter rim encases her shoulders and head. Lithophane of Bavaria in front of Ruhmeshalle. Twin domes thumblift.

NO MARKS.

Fig. 377

Fig. 378

MUNICH CHILD. 1 liter porcelain, 10'' (25.4 cm). 1/2 liter porcelain, 8½'' (20.9 cm).

They appear with black habit and pointed cowl. The yellow scapular starts at her neck, dropping to her slippers. "Gruss aus München" appears on the lower border. Cowl and sleeve linings are blue gray, slippers are red. The Child wears an "old maid" expression on some steins. She holds a bunch of radishes in her left hand, a book in her right. No pewter rim. A lithophane of the Statue of Bavaria.

NO MARKINGS.

166

MUNICH CHILD. 1 liter porcelain. Height varies from 9½"
to 11¼" (24-28 cm).

Identical to preceding, except pewter rim is missing
around shoulders. The shoulders on this and prior steins
look padded. Similar lithophane.

NO MARKINGS.

Fig. 379

Fig. 380

MUNICH CHILD. 1/2 liter porcelain, 8" (20.3 cm). 1/3
liter porcelain, 6¾" (17 cm). 1/4 liter porcelain, 6¼" (16.5
cm).

Coloring of this stein varies from piece to piece. The
robe and cowl have been noted in rust brown to dark
brown. The large scapular is generally cream color. Cowl
linings appear in yellow and brown. The Child holds a
foaming stein in its right hand. Two radishes are tucked
under the left. On some pieces, a blue or purple Bible is
held in the left hand, on others a beaker. The Child's face
shows a most cheerful expression. The lid is encased in a
rim of high quality pewter. Thumblifts have been noted in
various designs, most common, of course, being the twin
domes of Frauenkirche.

NO MARKS.

MUNICH CHILD. 1/2 liter porcelain. 11½" (28.5 cm).

The lining of the cowl and frontispiece (scapular) are
gold leaf. This Child has a stein in her right hand and the
usual radish in the left. The crumpled scapular seems to be
windswept at its lower border. The lithophane depicts a
building.

NO MARKINGS.

Fig. 381

Fig. 382

MUNICH CHILD. 1 liter earthenware. 12" (30.5 cm).

This stein has a highly glazed black robe, a yellow surplice, and red-lined sleeves. On the surplice is "Gruss aus München" (Greetings from Munich). The right hand holds a beige, silver-lidded HB stein, and the left holds two radishes. A pewter rim encases its head. The lining of the cowl is in gold leaf, the face is flesh-toned, and it has brown hair.

On bottom No. 117 A. NO MARKINGS.

Fig. 383

MUNICH CHILD. 1/2 liter earthenware. 8" (20 cm).

It is somewhat different from the usual Mayer and Reinemann steins. The black robe is trimmed in gold, and the handle beige with black stripe. The face wears a gleeful expression and is highly colored. She holds a foaming stein of beer in her left hand, a bunch of radishes in her right arm. A gold apron is bunched up over the radishes. Her cuff linings and base are red.

On bottom GERMANY and No. 1466. NO MARKINGS.

MUNICH CHILD. 1/2 liter earthenware. 7'' (17.7 cm).

A cream-colored stein of a roly-poly Child on a small base. The robe and cowl are glossy black, the cross shaped scapular is yellow with red cuff linings and slippers. The left hand holds a small red Bible, in the right a lidded foaming beer stein. The face is flesh-toned, the eyes looking upward, the hair is dark.

On the bottom the letters DRGM (3) and No. 154927. Also mold No. 695 B, Gesetzlich geschutzt.

Fig. 384

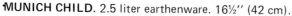

MUNICH CHILD. 2.5 liter earthenware. 16½'' (42 cm).

This tall, slender Child has a black robe and cowl, a yellow green to gold scapular and base, and red cuff linings and slippers. A wide open, foamy stein of beer is held in the right hand. The left hand holds a red book. Hands and a lifelike face are flesh colored, the hair is brown. A pewter rim encases the head.

Similar to the above stein are the letters DRGM 154927 (3). Mold No. 729 Germany and Gesetzlich geschutzt are also incised.

Fig. 386

Fig. 385

MUNICH CHILD. 1/4 liter stoneware. 5½'' (13 cm).

The smooth, tapering body and round cowl are painted black. Its face and hands, which hold a gray stein in the right and radishes in the left, are outlined in black and painted with various colors. A pewter rim encases shoulders and head. The painted scapular is yellow, linings of cowl and cuffs red, hair brown. The stein is reminiscent of Germany's Art Moderne period. Steins of this size were commonly used by children for festive affairs (see Figurals).

Decoration by J. REINEMANN (13).

169

MUNICH CHILD. 2.5 liter pottery. 19" (48.3 cm).

At the opposite extreme we find one of the largest of the *Kindl* seen by the author. It measures 19" from its base to the tip of the cowl. Its serene face is in skin-tones to contrast with the black of the robe and cowl. The cream surplice has a view of the twin towers of Frauenkirche on a shield held by the Child. The scroll at the base is inscribed, "So lang das drunt' am Platzl no' steht das Hofbräuhaus so lang geht auch den Münchnern d' Gemütlichkeit net aus" (As long as the Hofbrauhaus stands down at the "Platzl" will Gemütlichkeit of the Munichers remain).

NO MARKS.

Fig. 387

MUNICH CHILD. 3/10 liter earthenware. 6¼" (15.8 cm).

This Munich Child is short and round, with black robe and pointed cowl. Scapular is tan, as is the broad, belt-like band across the front on which the words "Gruss aus München" can be seen, along with the Bavarian rhombus crest. Child holds an HB stein and a plate of food, a radish tucked under one arm. Cowl lining maroon. Flesh-tone face has a boyish expression. Lid is pewter rimmed.

Made by REINHOLD MERKELBACH (5a). Mold number 551 impressed.

Fig. 388

Fig. 389

MUNICH CHILD. 1/2 liter earthenware. 8" (20.5 cm).

The Child wears a black robe and cowl, while the cowl lining may be maroon or blue. The scapular and belt are light tan to cream. The Child holds a platter of fried chicken in its left hand. Only Reinhold-Merkelbach made this humorous version. In the right hand is a HB stein with radishes tucked under the arm. Outlines of Munich's Frauenkirche can be seen, along with "Greetings from Munich". A pewter rim encases the head.

Made by REINHOLD MERKELBACH (5a). Mold number 323, Geschutzt.

MUNICH CHILD. 1/2 liter earthenware. 7¼" (18.4 cm).

The Child wears a black robe and cowl with a yellow surplice. HB stein has "Greetings from Munich". Radishes are in the left hand.

NO MARKINGS other than No. 117 G impressed.

Fig. 390

Fig. 391

MUNICH CHILD. 1/2 liter earthenware. 8½" (21.5 cm).

The body of stein is similar to above. However, there is a different face and pointed cowl. The Child has brown hair with a rosy, cheerful face.

The bottom is impressed with the same number 117 and the mark (unknown):

Fig. 392

MUNICH CHILD. 1 liter stoneware. 11" (27.9 cm).

High relief sleeves, three steins, and a bunch of radishes are added to the smooth, salt-glazed body with cobalt blue HB letters incised in the middle. A pewter rim encases the finely modeled head which may be porcelain or earthenware. The sleeves, shoulders, and cowl are black, the cuff linings gold. Cowl lining is gold leaf, face flesh-toned with rosy cheeks and red lips, and a strand of dark hair falling over the forehead.

Mold number 1285 impressed in bottom.

MUNICH CHILD. 1 liter stoneware. 11½" (29 cm).

The tan body is identical to preceding stein, except for red cuff linings. The head is different. Pointed cowl gives additional length to stein. No pewter rim.

The same mold number 1285 GERMANY is impressed in bottom. This stein evidently was made by the same manufacturer of number 1286 (see Monkeys).

Fig. 393

MUNICH CHILD. 1/2 liter earthenware. 9¼" (23.5 cm).

Unlike most of the squat and rotund versions, this *Münchner Kindl* is tall and elongated. In the right hand there is a plain stein with a flat lid. In the left there is a large radish. The cowled head, sitting on a pewter rim, makes up the stein cover. The texture of the garment is made from a great many etched wavy lines. The colors are black etched lines on a cream colored stein. A small amount of green glaze applied to the leaves of the radish is the only variation in the color scheme. A shiny overglaze covers the entire stein.

The under surface of the pewter ring bears the marking Reichs Zinn (a grade of pewter) with a MR underneath. The M & R refers to MARZI & REMY (9). The mold no. 314 is incised in the bottom of the base.

Fig. 394

MUNICH CHILD. 3/10 liter porcelain. 6¾" (17 cm).

The Child sitting atop this light beige barrel is holding a foaming stein and radishes. The handle is a radish on the bottom with leaves forming the handle.

NO MARKS or lithophane.

Fig. 395

BARREL. 1/2 liter porcelain. 8½" (21.5 cm).

The barrel is cream colored with the same handle as above. A pewter rim encases the inlaid lid on which another barrel is mounted. Astride this barrel sits a barefooted Munich Child, holding aloft a stein and some radishes. Its robe is brown.

The markings read MUSTERSCHUTZ (10). The lithophane shows the countryside with a small river and Munich in the background.

Fig. 396

BARREL. 1/2 liter porcelain. 8" (20.3 cm).

Similar to prior steins. However, this Child has a gray cat crawling down its right shoulder — perhaps reaching for the extended stein of beer? The handle is similar, with a lithophane depicting a city scene.

Marked MUSTERSCHUTZ (10) and the HASH mark (1).

Fig. 397

Fig. 398

BARREL. 1/2 liter porcelain. 8½'' (21.5 cm).

Similar to the prior steins, Here the Child is holding a radish high in the air. The staves of the barrel are beige with black bands. Similar handle to the prior steins. Pewter thumblift depicts the twin towers of Munich. Lithophane of the Statue of Bavaria.

Marked MARTIN PAUSON (14).

Old Coat of Arms

New Coat of Arms

Artist's rendition of a modern Munich Child

174

Fig. 399

MUNICH CHILD. Pewter. 7½″ (19 cm).

The Child is made entirely of heavy grade pewter. It holds a large open stein in the left hand; two radishes, one of them inverted, are in the right hand.

There are NO MARKS to indicate a manufacturer. The initials JRM are incised in the pin of the pewter hinge of the thumblift.

SKULLS

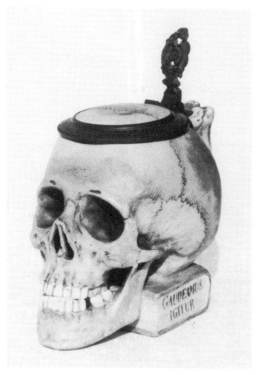

SKULL. 1/2 liter bisque porcelain. 5½'' (14 cm). 1/3 liter, 4¼'' (10.7 cm).

Here we find an anatomically correct rendition of a human skull. It is resting on the *Commersbuch* which is inscribed with the Latin ''Gaudeamus Igitur, juvenes dum sumus'' (Let us therefore rejoice while we are still young . . . soon the soil will have us). (For further information about this drinking song, look under :''Yowling Cat on Book'' in Animals section.) Color is a bone white with finely detailed beige sutures. The handle is in the shape of a bone.

A similar version to this 1/2 liter stein has an enlarged book which can be used for a music box.

Bottom of stein has impressed anchor mark of E. BOHNE SOEHNE (2a) and mold number 9136/3.

Fig. 400

Fig. 401

176

Fig. 402

SKULL. Bisque 1/2 liter, 5'' (12.7 cm). 1/3 liter, 3¾'' (9.6 cm).

This stein is very similar in worksmanship and coloring to the prior steins. However, the book is not present. It should be noted that these skulls have been seen with different tooth arrangements.

Marked E. BOHNE SOEHNE (2a). Very often no mark appears on these steins.

SKULL. 1/2 liter porcelain. 5'' (12.7 cm).

Similar in texture to the last stein. This skull varies in the shape of the unique handle. It extends back to give the skull a length of 7½'' (19 cm).

NO MARKS.

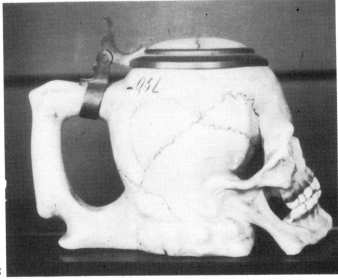

Fig. 403

177

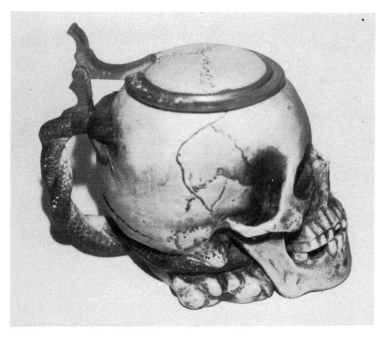

Fig. 404

SKULL. 1/2 liter bisque porcelain. 4¾" (12.1 cm).

Very unusual skull with caduceus (entwined serpents) handle. The bone white coloring is similar to the prior steins.

NO MARKS, only mold No. 695.

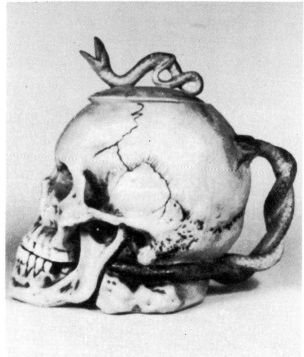

SKULL. 1/2 liter bisque porcelain. 6½" (16.5 cm).

Very similar to the prior stein. Again we see the caduceus handle, but there is no attachment to the serpent-lined lid. This possibly was used as a tobacco container. Coloring is basically an off-white, except for the reddish-brown serpents on the handle.

NO MARKS.

Fig. 405

SKULL. 1/2 liter glazed porcelain.

This skull has a unique thumblift depicting a soldier riding a rearing horse. The eye of the horse has a lithophane insert: when held to the light it reveals a scene of a military academy. This regimental-type skull is dated 1908/11.

NO MARKS.

Fig. 406

BACK TO BACK SKULLS. 4/10 liter pottery. 5¼'' (13.3 cm).

This bisque is unique in that the two faces are on opposite sides of the stein. The bone-shaped handle divides it on one side and crossed scythes on the front. Laurel leaves are evident under the mandibles of both faces. Coloring is an off-white.

NO MARKS.

Fig. 407

179

Fig. 408

HALF SATAN-HALF SKULL. 1/2 liter. 6" (15.2 cm).

Similar to the prior stein, here we see the head of Satan in varying shades of red orange highlights. His horns are incorporated into his portion of the pewter lined lid. Opposite is the bone-white coloring of the skull, with its corresponding smooth cranium in the lid. The Satan has a devilish look to his detailed face, similar to the next steins. This stein is also found in the 1/4 liter and 3/10 liter sizes.

Marked E. BOHNE SOEHNE (2a).

Fig. 409

Fig. 410

Fig. 411

Fig. 412

SATAN. 1/2 liter bisque porcelain. 6¼'' (15.8 cm). Also available in 1/4 liter size.

This stein is in the shape of an evil Satan head. A hideous smile reveals fang-like teeth. Wart-like protrubances are found scattered around his face. Hanging from his ears are pierced gold rings. Two horns project from the pewter ringed lid. A flowing goatee enhances his evil countenance, and swirled hair makes up the rear of the stein and the handle. An ornate thumblift rises above the stein. A bisque finish enriches the subtle red-brown-black tones of the devil's face. The tips of the horns, eye pupils, and the teeth are stark white. The green eyes give the figure a strikingly sinister look.

Marked E. BOHNE SOEHNE (2a).

181

Fig. 413

MEPHISTO. 1/2 liter glazed porcelain. 8'' (20.3 cm).

This most unusual characterization of Satan has many lifelike features. His skin-toned face has a toothy and sinister grin. A deep brown Tyrolean hat sits on top his head to form the lid. A red and black cowl blends behind his head to form the handle.

Marked MUSTERSCHUTZ (10) and the HASH (1) mark. The numbers 110/323 were noted on the base.

SATAN. 1/2 liter pottery. 7½'' (19 cm) to the top of the pewter lid.

This humorous stein has the devil with a sly smile on his face. Colored a light beige with red lips and dark eyes, he looks off to the side. Two small horns protrude from his forehead; behind them his hair is composed of red and green hops.

Marked MERKELBACH & WICK (4-d).

SATAN. 1/2 liter pottery. 6½'' (16.5 cm).

A brownish mate to the preceding stein. It appears to be from same mold, however, this devil's lid forms his forehead. Again we see the hops leaves in the hair.

Marked MERKELBACH & WICK (4d). Mold No. 2601.

Fig. 414

Fig. 415

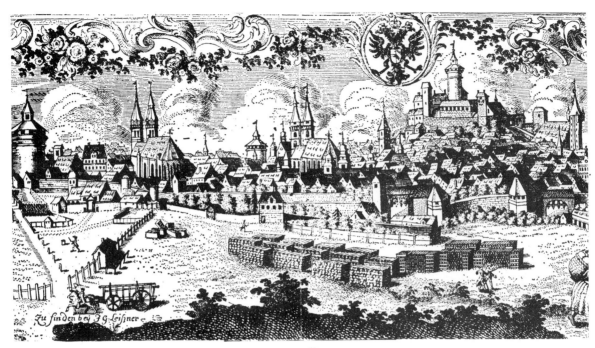

OLD NÜRNBERG

DÜRERTURM TOWER. 1/2 liter pottery. 9½" (24.1 cm). to the top of the flag on top of the conical roof-shaped pewter lid. (NOTE: Some specimens appear to have been manufactured without a flag.)

This stein is a replica of the Nurnberg Tower known as the Dürerturm (formerly the Spittlertorturm or Spittler Gate Tower). This tower is one of the four great round tower gates within the walls of Old Nurnberg. The above picture shows two of them. The body of the stein is beige with brown incised brick mortar. There are circular blue scenes etched on either side. The stein was made with a variety of scenes, including: a relief of Hans Sach, famous Meistersinger; a 4F scene; and various scenes of the city of Nurnberg.

In the rear of the stein, under the handle, is the inscription "Gruss aus Nürnberg" (Greetings from Nurnberg). The pewter thumblift is a figure of the Gooseman.

Interestingly, this same stein has been seen with the following marks: T. W. GESETZLICH GESCHUZT; MARZI & REMI (9a); and F & M No. 1190.

N

Fig. 416

183

TOWER. 1/4 liter pottery. 8¼" (20.9 cm) to the tip of the pewter flag.

Similar to prior tower in coloring. This smaller, rarer version has panels on either side showing two different scenes of Nürnberg.

Marked F & M GESETZL GESCHÜZT mold No. 6019.
N

Fig. 417

TOWER. 1/2 liter pewter. 9½" (24.1 cm).

Very similar to the previously described pottery steins, this stein is complete with gallery, windows, smoke stack, and flag. Stones are "etched" into the body for a very realistic appearance. Circular side panels have etched views of old Nurnberg. The internal portion of the stein is silver plate.

Marked F & M
N

Fig. 418

Fig. 419

FRAUENKIRCHE TOWER. 1/2 liter salt glaze stoneware. 8½'' (21.5 cm).

The pewter lid makes up the famed "Onion" dome. There are three tiers of the tower represented. The uppermost has small windows, the middle section has louvered portals, and the lower tier has three clocks, all set at 3:02. The magnificent pewter thumblift has a *Münchner Kindl* in relief on a stylized shield. At the child's left foot is a bit of the checkered insignia of Munich. On the right foot side is the monogram ![monogram] The building material is block.

A manganese color is used extensively, save for the blue color on the clocks and a ring around the base. The gray color makes up the stein body.

The famed Frauenkirche (Church of Our Lady) is one of Munich's most famous landmarks. Rising from the church is a pair of these onion domed towers.

Marked T. W. GESETZLICH GESCHÜTZT. This stein is also seen in the 1 liter size measuring 11'' (27.9 cm).

185

Fig. 420

FRAUENKIRCHE TOWER. 1/2 liter porcelain.

A more stylized and detailed version of the previously described stein, here the body is a rich red brown and white. The base is black, with shields on the left and right. The front panel shows an enameled Munich child. The "onion" lid is green shading to black (giving the appearance of an old tarnished dome). The stein is obviously hand painted. The body has a rough unsymmetrical appearance.

On the rear of the stein below the handle is the mark MARTIN PAUSON MÜNCHEN, GES-ETZL GESCHÜTZT N126. A large lithophane of the Bavaria Statue is on the base.

LITHOPHANE

ST. PETER'S CHURCH (Munich). 1 liter salt glaze pottery. 13" (32.9 cm) to the tip of the spire.

This unique clock tower is set off by the beauty of the pewter lid. The body of the stein is gray with blue details in the windows and clocks. The thumblift is a Munich maid.

A blue ledge under the upper windows has the inscription "So lang der alte Peter, der Petersthurm noch steht" (As long as St. Peter's stands in Munich, Gemütlicheit will not die out!)

The Parish Church of St. Peter is the oldest church in Munich (1278-1294). The center tower (known as "Old Peter") dates from the 14th century.

NO MARKS, only GESETZLICH GESCHÜTZT.

Fig. 421

Fig. 422

SALZBURG TOWER. 1/2 liter pottery. 11" (27.9 cm).

The body and lid form the tower. The upper tier houses openings showing racks of bells. The middle tier is pillared and has round portals. A tile roof separates the middle tier from the main body of the tower. The upper portion of the lower section houses a series of clocks that are set at 11:15. Windows make up the lowest portion of the stein.

The inscription "Gruss aus Salzburg" (Greetings from Salzburg) is printed around the base. The back of the handle has edelweiss blossoms on it. A lyre thumblift completes the decoration. The body of the stein is cream, with a black glaze for details. A touch of brown is used in the centers of the edelweiss.

A large false bottom contributes to its 11" height. Holes for the attachment of a music box are present.

This tower is located on the main square in Salzburg, Austria.

NO MARKS, only GESETZL. GESCHÜTZT.

TOWER. 1/2 liter salt glaze stoneware. 8¾'' (22.2 cm).

This stein is in the shape of a church and tower. The body of the tower is ceramic and the lid dome is pewter. The architecture of the building is typically Romanesque. The building appears to be built of blocks. A heraldic crest makes up the thumblift. A pewter cross tops off the beautiful pewter dome. A color scheme of manganese (violet) and gray accounts for the stein's detail.

It resembles Elizabethenkirche (St. Elizabeth's Church) in Nurnberg.

NO MARKS.

Fig. 423

CASTLE TOWER. 1 liter pewter. 16'' (40.6 cm).

A very large, unusual depiction of a tower. A man is seen on the top parapet and a woman on the front balcony.

NO MARKS on this very rare stein.

Fig. 424

Fig. 425

Fig. 426

CLOCK TOWER. 1/2 liter pottery. 10¼″ (26.1 cm).

This unusual square stein has a pedestal base. A scene on three sides shows a clock with a smiling face. The time reads 1:15. The front side says, "Früh Morgens wenn die Hähne krähn, dann Wollen wir nach Hause Gehn" (Early in the morning, when the rooster crows, that's the time to go home).

The lid is the roof of the clock tower with its bell tower cupola on top. Two pigeons are sitting on the lid, while a fox sneaks up the handle. A rooster and a hen are seen along the base. Colors are beige and brown with a blue roof.

A similar stein appears in a glazed pottery with reds appearing on the onion domed cupola, face of the clocks, and the base.

NO MARKS, only mold No. 11299 GERMANY.

Fig. 427

TOWER. 1/2 liter porcelain. 11'' (27.9 cm).

An unidentified building. The body of the stein is salmon colored with brown corners. The windows on all four level are black. A plain white handle is topped by an ornate, delicate, pewter thumblift of flowers and leaves. This stein has a lithophane of a man on a bicycle.

NO MARKS.

ALLIGATORS

Fig. 428

Fig. 429

WRAP AROUND ALLIGATOR. 1/2 liter porcelain. 6" (15.2 cm).

This delicate alligator in bas relief encircles the body of the stein, which represents a body of water. The scaly green tail forms the handle and extends through the lid as though it is coming out of the water. The water is colored light blue, white, and gray. The alligator is in varying shades of blacks and greens, with a tan underbelly.

Many German manufacturing firms made alligator motif steins to be sold in Florida in the early 1900s as souvenirs. From 1895 to 1905, Florida celebrated many significant anniversaries: its 50th year as a state; 100 years since becoming a territory (West Florida); 100th anniversary of Fort Marion and the draining of the famous Everglades.

NO MARKS.

SITTING ALLIGATOR. 1/8 liter pottery. 6" (15.2 cm).

This upright alligator appears to be atop a stand of some sort, perhaps a circus stand. The tail loops upward to form the handle of the stein. The figure is tinted varying shades of green, the underbelly is yellow, and the base is brown and tan. A matte finish gives the character a bisque appearance, save for the base which has a shiny overglaze.

Marked MARZI and REMI (9b) and the mold No. 1914.

191

Fig. 430

SITTING ALLIGATOR. 1/2 liter porcelain. 7'' (17.7 cm).

    The reputation of this species is one of ferocity, but this can't be the case with this appealing alligator. The character is posed with a winning smile and a nonchalant toss of his tail over his foreleg. The loop of the tail serves as the handle for the stein. The dorsal portion of the alligator's body varies from stein to stein. While some examples are of a light olive green and brown, others possess deep forest green hues. Underbelly portions are usually a cream color. A plain pewter thumblift is affixed to the head and handle.

    Marked MUSTERSCHUTZ (10) and the HASH (1) mark.

Fig. 431

FISH. 1/2 liter pottery. 9" (22.9 cm).

Eleven herrings, tails down, make up the body of this gaily colored stein. A cat and monkey poke their heads out between the tightly packed fish to peer at one another. A monkey's head appears in relief on the curved part of the handle.

Occasionally this stein is seen with a special cast pewter cat as a thumblift. A verse around the base reads, "Den grössten kater lehrt erfahrung, bezwingt ein guter saurer Harung" (Experience teaches that a good sour herring cures the biggest hangover).

Marked REINHOLD MERKELBACH (5a) and mold No. 1152.

FROG. 1/2 liter porcelain. 6'' (15.2 cm).

Sitting in an upright position, this green speckled frog ponders some unknown thought. Two gilt eyes rolled back and a toe pad on his chin enhance this pose. A pale green underbelly finishes out the color scheme of this engaging character. The handle is a rolled green lily pad. Attaching the handle to the frog's head is a plain pewter thumblift.

Marked MUSTERSCHUTZ (10) and the HASH (1) mark.

Fig. 432

FROG. 1/2 liter porcelain. 6'' (15.2 cm).

A similar figure to the above, but this one has a blue six-pointed star on his belly.

Fig. 433

HEIDELBERG FROG DUELIST. 1/2 liter porcelain. 7'' (17.7 cm).

Dressed in the garb of a student dueling society, this frog, with his arms folded and chin uplifted, strikes a cocky pose to his would-be challenger. His cap, club ribbon, and scar are all evidence of his membership in a dueling fraternity. Attached to his belt are some other accessories: a key, pipe, and strap.

The stein is richly colored with white and honey tones commonly associated with the MUSTERSCHUTZ (10) markings. While some examples of this stein are without markings on the base, others have the word BAVARIA glazed stamped.

Fig. 434

FROG. 1/2 liter porcelain. 7½" (19 cm).

This most docile frog is sporting a small red and black cap. His underbelly is a soft white to blend in with the green tones of his crouched hind legs.

NO MARKS.

Fig. 435

FROG AS ROMAN COMMANDER-IN-CHIEF. 1/2 liter pottery. 8" (20.3 cm).

A stern frog, he sports several different red medallions across his chest.

NO MARKS on the base, only the mold No. 27, which is identified in DÜMLER & BREIDEN (19). The following inscription is on its back: SCHUTZ DLB MARKE

Fig. 436

GENTLEMAN FROG. Pottery 1/2 liter. 8" (20.3 cm).

This colorful frog is sporting a brown and gray fedora to top off his brown waist coat and Bavarian pipe. Across his mid-section is a gray scroll which says, "Willst du nicht dem Frosche gleich im Sumpf versinken steige in Gambrinus Reich wo volle humpen winken" (If you don't want to sink into the swamp, like a frog climb into the Gambrinus empire where full mugs beckon).

NO MARKS, only mold No. 973 GERMANY.

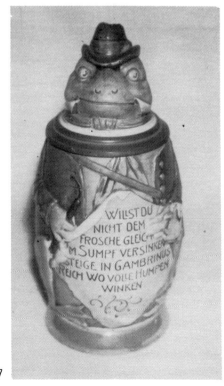

Fig. 437

195

Fig. 438

FROG. 1/2 liter pottery. 6½" (16.5 cm).

Crouched on his hind legs, this guy is casually strumming on his brown banjo.

Colored varying shades of green. There are no manufacturers marks, only mold No. 1429.

FROG. 1/2 liter pottery. 7¼" (18.4 cm).

A simple frog, squatting in the green marshes, has his short forelegs spread to reveal the webbing. On his chest is written, "Der Frosch quackt wenn er sich labt" (The frog croaks when he is enjoying himself). He is colored in shades of green and also in varying hues of yellows and greens.

NO MARKS, only mold No. 825 GERMANY.

Fig. 439

196

Fig. 440

HOUSE. 1/2 liter stoneware. 6½" (16.5 cm).

A very rare, unusual rectangular stein. The lid of the house is the brown thatched roof and the brick red chimney. The front of the house has a wooden door and shuttered windows. Along the left side can be seen a young man climbing a ladder to meet his girl friend. She is leaning out the window to hold his hand. The opposite side of the house shows a little gray dog frolicking in the grass. A brown tree trunk composes the handle of this beautiful stein.

NO MARKS only No. 1777 GERMANY.

Fig. 441

HOUSE. 1/2 liter pottery. 8'' (20 cm).

Here we see a circular house, with Cupid climbing in the window on the side. The front door is slightly ajar, showing the father waiting with a stick in his hand. The brick red conical lid has three very small windows shaped like birdhouses. The bricks of the walls are cream. An owl thumblift sits atop the handle. The pottery handle is shaped like a tree trunk. The lithophane shows the Munich Maid with *"Prosit"* along the top edge.

Incised in the pewter is PAUSON on one side, MÜN-CHEN on the other. NO MARKS.

Fig. 442

PRETZEL. 1/2 liter porcelain. 6'' (15.2 cm).

One of the few unconventional steins produced by VILLEROY and BOCH, the vessel consists of a stack of pretzels. A twisted pretzel projects from the inlaid lid, and the same type of pretzel forms an interesting two-holed handle. The stein is colored in the rich russet colors of natural pretzels.

The V & B castle mark (16b) is incised in the bottom, along with No. 2388.

Fig. 443

Fig. 444

ZUGSPITZE. 1/2 liter stoneware. 8'' (20 cm).

Germany's highest peak, the Zugspitze, is the subject of this stein. The body of the brightly colored stein is crafted into the shape of a rugged mountain. Circling the stein is a trail that meanders past farms, lakes, and lodges, until it arrives at the summit. Rising from the topmost crag is a pewter cross; on some examples a flag flies from the mountain top. A large rock with the inscription Zugspitze Gipfel proclaims the summit of the peak. The pewter thumblift is in the shape of a chamois' head.

An oval on the bottom encloses the name MARTIN PAUSON, MÜNCHEN (14). Also GESETLICH GES-CHUTZ.

Fig. 445

NURNBERG FUNNEL. 1/2 liter, 7'' (17.7 cm). 1/4 liter, 5½'' (14 cm).

This popular funnel-shaped stein was produced in two sizes. The funnel portion is commonly colored gray. Much rarer is a yellow hued body. On the front are the words "Nürnberger trichter" in fancy black and red script. An impish jester in a stooped position forms the handle. His garb is brilliantly colored in crimson and black, with gold leaf trim. The smirking knave appears to be peeking around the stein with his hand cupped to his ear, trying to catch any idle gossip.

Gracing the bottom of the stein is an exquisite lithophane of the Gooseman Fountain statue, located in front of the Rathaus in Nurnberg. (Other steins depicting the Gooseman can be found in Figurals.)

Marked MUSTERSCHUTZ (10) and HASH (1).

DER GÄNSEMÄNNCHENBRUNNEN

LITHOPHANE

199

Schuentzenliesl (shooting contests) were very common in rural towns and villages of old Bavaria. It was usually an annual event to see who was the best marksman and was looked forward to throughout the year. These contests were akin to the turkey shoots that used to be held in America. It was also a "King-of-the-mountain" type of contest. Many steins relating to these contests depict a girl wearing a hat similar to a target. One of the most common target steins is the V & B Mettlach No. 1526/1076.

MARKSMAN. 1/2 liter pottery. 10" (25.4 cm).

This figure is sporting a black and white target on his hat band. His hat and coat are a dark blue, his skin a light beige, his rifle is black.

Marked J. REINEMANN MÜNCHEN (13). GESETLICHT GESCHUTZT.

Fig. 446

TARGET BARREL. 1/2 liter porcelain. 7" (17.7 cm).

Popping out of the lid is the body of a jester holding a target. The stein has crossed guns in relief on the front, a man on one side, and a woman holding an open stein on the other.

The usual brown/beige colors are seen on this unique stein. Lithophane depicts a mountain with trees.

Marked MUSTERSCHUTZ (10).

TARGET LADY. 1/2 liter porcelain. 6" (15.2 cm) to the top of the black and white target.

Her reddish brown hair is braided in the back to form the handle. Colors are light beige and creams.

NO MARKS, only GESETLICHT GESCHUTZT.

Fig. 447

Fig. 448

Fig. 449

KEEPER OF THE WINE. 1/2 liter porcelain. 8½" (22.5 cm).

Standing on top of the large keg is the wine cellar keeper. In his left hand is a silver wine goblet, and dangling from his shoulder we see the silver key. This figure is very similar to the "Perkeo" described in Figurals.

Along the staves is the inscription, "Alt Heidelberg du feine" (Old Heidelberg, you fine city). The lithophane depicts a city scene, possibly Heidelberg.

Coloring of this stein is the beige/brown associated with the HASH (1) and MUSTER-SCHUTZ (10) marks.

Fig. 450

DWARF. 1/2 liter porcelain. 7¾" (19.7 cm).

Sitting atop the barrel is a tiny white dwarf, imbibing from a large goblet. The pale green staves make a striking contrast to the gold bands that encircle the barrel.

NO MARKS.

Fig. 451

Fig. 452

CAVALIER. 1/2 liter earthenware. 7½" (19 cm).

The body of this stein is of a white glazed earthenware. Raised barley and hops decorate the sides of the vessel. In some examples of this stein, the relief beer ingredients are gold lustered, while in others the background is colored and the raised portions are white. The porcelain lid is encircled by a pewter ring with a small nub for a thumblift. Sitting, with a large book across his lap, is a cavalier. The colors of this tiny figure vary from stein to stein: in some the man is gaily attired, while in others he is tinted with shades of tan and white. The bearded figure is lifting high a glass. Strapped across the cavalier's back is a large drinking horn.

NO MARKS.

TIPSY CAVALIER. 1/2 liter porcelain. 7½'' (19 cm).

Sitting with his pokal of beer between his outstretched legs, our drunken cavalier is wearing a funnel hat. The entire lid is a deep brown in color. The base consists of the well known variegated beige and brown barrel stein.

Marked VILLEROY AND BOCH (16a) No. 675.

Fig. 453

BEEHIVE. 1/2 liter pottery. 7¼'' (18.4 cm).

An old-fashioned, straw, woven beehive has many small bees scattered about in relief. The small opening to the hive is at the front of the base. Two red, heart-shaped panels on either side of the hive contain the following verses from a folk song that was popular among German soliders at the turn of the century: "Mein Herz das ist ein Bienenhaus, die Mädchen darin das sind die Bienen" (My heart is a beehive, the girls in it are the bees); and, on the other side, "Sie fliegen ein, sie fliegen aus gerad wie einem Bienehaus" (They fly in, they fly out, just like in a beehive). The handle also carries out the woven straw style of the hive.

NO MARKS, only mold No. 1384 D incised in the base.

Fig. 454

ROOK. 1/2 liter pottery. 8'' (20.3 cm).

The game of chess is represented by this salt glazed rook. The stone tower is colored with a fine manganese glaze to give the stein a violet tint. Rising out of the pewter ring, at the top of the pedestaled tower, is a chess board imprinted on its floor. A large pewter horse's head thumblift (chess knight) overlooks the rook.

Marked J. REINEMANN MÜNCHEN (13); also GESETZ-LICH GESCHÜTZT impressed in the bottom.

Fig. 455

MUSHROOM. 1/2 liter porcelain. 7¾" (19.7 cm).

In this fanciful representation of a toadstool, we see a bearded elf perched atop the rust colored mushroom cap which forms the lid. The honey toned elf gazes out at the world from this vantage point. Wearing a peaked cap, he sits with his hands clasped around his crossed legs. The handle is unique as it is formed from the linked bodies of two other dwarfs. A plain pewter thumblift joins the dwarfs' bodies with the mushroom cap. The shaft of this fleshy mushroom is cream colored. The two dwarfs of the handle are dark beige, with light beige coloring in the face and hands. The beards are cream. Another fine feature of this vessel is a scene of deer drinking from a mountain spring in the beautiful lithophane in the base.

Marked with the blue HASH (1) mark and the green MUSTERSCHUTZ (10).

Fig. 456

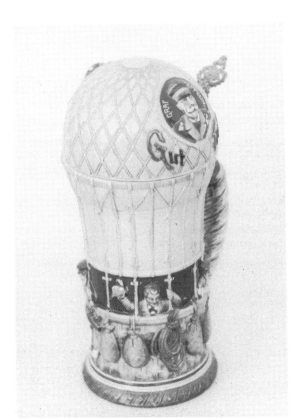

Fig. 457

HOT AIR BALLOON. 1/2 liter pottery. 9½" (24 cm).

A very large, relief likeness of a hot air balloon. The yellow balloon forms the lid of this most unusual stein. On one side is a relief likeness of *Graf* Zeppelin; on the other side is one of Orville Wright. Under Zeppelin is the inscription "Gut Flug" (Good flight). The yellow and brown wicker basket has ropes, sandbags, and an anchor hanging over its sides.

Four people can be seen standing in the basket. A man and woman wear Tyrolean dress. The pilot is using a telescope, and another man has binoculars. Green open-air spaces are seen behind the passengers.

This stein was probably made about 1910. Orville Wright made the first airplane flight demonstration at Templehof Field, Berlin, on September 10, 1909. The following week he flew there in the presence of the German Empress. In 1908 Zeppelin's airship was destroyed and a national fund raising (for a new ship) was in process in 1909.

The pewter thumblift is the likeness of a heavy rope. Below the rope-like handle is the mark 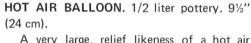 NO MARKS on base, only Mold

No. 1232 GERMANY.

BICYCLE. 1/2 liter porcelain. 6″ (15.2 cm).

The body of this bulbous shaped stein is flattened on the sides into spoked panels representing the wheels of a bicycle. A banderole inscribed "All heil" (the German cyclists' motto) covers the front. A pewter ring holds the inlaid lid with a raised shield of a two-wheeler. Positioned at the base of the curved handle is a small back wheel, similar to that found on the following high-wheeler. The large lithophane shows a scene of a young lad falling off his high-wheeler into a young woman, much to the delight of the onlooking children.

Marked MUSTERSCHUTZ (10).

Fig. 458

L.A.W. BICYCLE. 1/2 liter porcelain. 6¾″ (17 cm).

Only slight differences exist between this vessel and the preceding stein. The slogan on the banderole reads "L.A.W." These letters represent the League of American Wheelers, a popular bicycling society at the turn of the century. The porcelain shield on the lid is marked with the raised L.A.W. insignia. At least two different lithophanes are found in this stein. The most common is the same as in the last stein. The other view is of a couple slowly pedaling their bicycles down a curving lane. Both lithophanes are unusually large and measure over 3″ in diameter.

Colors of all the steins are beiges and browns, as associated with the marking MUSTERSCHUTZ (10).

Fig. 459

LITHOPHANES

204

HIGH WHEELER. 1/2 liter pewter and stoneware. 7¼″ (18.4 cm)

Commonly referred to as an 1860 Penny Farthing, the two-wheeler and its rider are ready for a ride. The drinking portion of the vessel is crafted of salt glazed stoneware colored a cobalt blue. Making up this portion are the deeply incised spoked high wheel and the rider's lower legs. Sitting astride the saddle is the cast body of the rider. A pewter shaft, attached to the top of the handle and extending below it, grips the small pewter back wheel. The mustached rider is dressed in the riding togs of the day, including hat.

The pewter lid is marked GESETZL GESCHÜTZT. NO MARKS on bottom.

Fig. 460

UMBRELLA. 1/2 liter porcelain 10″ (25.4 cm).

Four nattily attired gentleman crowded beneath a single pewter umbrella make this stein a real eyecatcher. The many examples of this stein show a variety of the colors and styles of the garments worn by the men. In some instances the same dude's trousers might be plain, striped, or checked. Other variations show up in the canes and top coats. The men are all wearing top hats, gloves, gold watches and fobs, and monacles in their right eye only. These men have a certain haughtiness about them, and it has been said they appear to be four college students out on the town. The crescent moon on the pewter thumblift is grinning down on them in a devilish manner, as though he knows they are up to no good.

This version has a 1½″ music box base. Other variations of this stein are 9″ (23 cm) in height and have two different lithophanes. One scene shows two dancers on stage with black top hats and canes; one dancer is smoking a cigar, and the other is attired in long black tails; both figures are holding their canes and top hats over their heads. The other lithophane is of a pair of clowns on a street, bowing to each other with tipped hats.

NO MARKS.

Fig. 461

ARMORED KNIGHT. 1/2 liter pottery. 9'' (23 cm).

This salt glazed knight is colored a deep Prussian blue. Emblazoned across the breast plate is the German Imperial Eagle. Running down each side of the figure is a stylized representation of the knight's mail used for protection of his arms. A snarling griffin clutches the visored helmet. The handle of the stein is fashioned from the knight's gauntlet holding a shield. The base of the stein has an oval mark:

Fig. 462

INSULATOR. 1/2 liter porcelain. 7'' (17.7 cm).

This deep cobalt blue stein has the appearance of an electrical insulator. A gold cable wraps around the neck of the stein. A gold crest appears on its front.

NO MARKS.

Fig. 463

Fig. 464

BOTTLE. 1/2 liter salt glaze pottery. 9'' (23 cm).

This blue and gray stein is in the shape of large bottle. In relief along the sides can be seen a cat and monkey climbing towards the top. Around them is a virtual sea of fish and sausages. A lizard lurks along the bottom edge. Oh, what a hangover the drinker will have tomorrow! The inscription: "Der Geist einmal heraufbeschworen lässt seine Folgen bald erkennen, den opfern die er sich erkoren an dingen die wir Affen, Kater nennen" (Once the spirit has been summoned, he'll soon show his intent to the victims whom he chooses and which are the things we call monkeys, tomcats — hangovers).

NO MARKS, only GES. GESCH. LB & C

BOTTLE. 1/2 liter pottery. 9½" (24 cm).

This is a more colorful version of the previous stein, showing a red monkey and cat climbing the sides. The body and lid are filled with red sausages, blue fishes, and white radishes. A red devil handle is peering up at the ram, which has its head inside the spout of the bottle. What a nightmare!

This stein has the same inscription and marks as the previous one.

Fig. 465

Fig. 466

DRAWSTRING BAG OF MONEY. 1/2 liter porcelain. 7" (17.7 cm).

An unusual depiction of a money bag. The grayish body has an arm reaching out and around to form the handle. The white side panel is "attached" with four red buttons marked *TW*. The philosophical inscription is, "Wer nichts erheirathet und nichts erbt. Der bleibt ein armes Luder bis er sterbt!" (He who does not marry money and does not inherit anything remains a poor devil until he dies).

NO MARKS, only No. 75.

DRUNK. 1/2 liter porcelain. 7" (17.7 cm).

This tipsy fellow appears to be sitting inside the keg. The lid is formed by his immersed torso. However, his black boots are attached to the base. The inscription along the side shows his feelings: "I ko nix dafür i war bald dasuffa im bayrischen Bier!" (Can't help it — I almost drowned in Bavarian beer!)

NO MARKS.

Fig. 467

Rubaiyat of Omar Khayyam; illustrated by Edmund J. Sullivan

PROSIT!

Rubaiyat of Omar Khayyam; illustrated by Edmund J. Sullivan

Rubaiyat of Omar Khayyam; illustrated by Edmund J. Sullivan

PROSIT!